"William James amusingly noted that oxide inhalation is increased understa phy. As fun as that sounds, I have a better suggestion: read this splendid book by Alex Tseng before diving into the German idealist's profoundly difficult writings. I learned many new and useful things from Tseng's well-informed exposition and analysis. Reformed readers will especially appreciate the discussion of how Bavinck, Vos, and Van Til 'salvaged treasures from Hegel's shipwreck,' exposing the flawed foundations of his system while co-opting his common-grace insights to demonstrate the virtues of a Reformed Christian worldview."

—**James N. Anderson**, Professor of Theology and Philosophy, Reformed Theological Seminary, Charlotte

"G. W. F. Hegel had an incalculable influence on the modern world. Whether faithfully or not, his philosophy was adopted by major thinkers as well as political activists throughout the nineteenth and twentieth centuries. His dictum that the rational alone is real was embodied in a progressive, organic view of history that culminates in an absolute state. China, Nazi Germany, the Soviet Union, and even parts of American liberalism stand on this pillar. Shao Kai Tseng's deeply learned account presents Hegel as an absolute realist whose views have found some echoes in Bavinck, Vos, Van Til, and even Schaeffer, and yet who is ultimately one of the great foes of biblical Christian faith. This series just keeps getting better and better."

—**William Edgar**, Professor of Apologetics, Westminster Theological Seminary

"Tseng's introduction to Hegel achieves a remarkable balance of clarity, depth, and intellectual charity. He manages to present the essential features of Hegel's thought in accessible and engaging terms (no small feat!), while resisting the temptation to caricature. He combines these virtues with a rich grasp of theological history to help us appreciate how one of modern philosophy's most important thinkers has been, and continues to be, both a challenge and an inspiration to the Reformed Christian tradition. This book represents the best of the genre, and will be of interest to both student and teacher."

—**Ryan Kemp**, Assistant Professor of Philosophy, Wheaton College

"Alex Tseng's book not only sets out a clear and reliable introduction to Hegel's thought but also makes clear why this is important to Christians—not least those who are inclined to view it with suspicion."

—**George Pattison**, 1640 Professor of Divinity, University of Glasgow; Fellow, Max Weber Centre for Advanced Research in Cultural and Social Studies

"In an era when nontheological and antimetaphysical readings of G. W. F. Hegel tend to dominate the scholarly scene, Shao Kai Tseng's concise and highly readable study contributes valuably to a resituation of Hegel in a theological light wherein he can be understood and assessed as he deserves to be. The explication of key themes in Hegel's absolute idealism is admirably lucid, and Tseng's 'Reformed assessment' successfully steers clear of any temptation to interpret Hegel in terms of 'friend or foe.' What's more, Tseng's exposition of the critical reception of Hegel by thinkers such as Herman Bavinck, Geerhardus Vos, Francis Schaeffer, and especially Cornelius Van Til might be particularly appreciated by readers interested in the Reformed tradition, but will prove valuable to anyone interested in genuinely theological assessments of Hegel. This is a welcome entry in historical theology and the history of philosophy."

—**Joel D. S. Rasmussen**, Mansfield College, University of Oxford

"No great philosopher presents his readers with more formidable obstacles than Hegel. It is a pleasure, then, to be able to give Alex Tseng's book a very warm welcome. Professor Tseng is an authoritative, approachable, engaged, and always fair-minded guide. The student coming to Hegel's thought for the first time is in excellent hands."
—**Michael E. Rosen**, Senator Joseph S. Clark Professor of Ethics in Politics and Government, Department of Government, Harvard University

"Alex Tseng's brilliant introduction to Hegel betrays on every page the author's impeccable grasp of his subject. Writing from the perspective of Reformed theology, Tseng makes a strong and plausible case for serious theological intellectual engagement with this uniquely influential thinker. Accessible and precise at the same time, the book is a highly rewarding read."
—**Johannes Zachhuber**, Professor of Historical and Systematic Theology, University of Oxford, Faculty of Theology and Religion

Praise for the Great Thinkers Series

"After a long eclipse, intellectual history is back. We are becoming aware, once again, that ideas have consequences. The importance of P&R Publishing's leadership in this trend cannot be overstated. The series Great Thinkers: Critical Studies of Minds That Shape Us is a tool that I wish I had possessed when I was in college and early in my ministry. The scholars examined in this well-chosen group have shaped our minds and habits more than we know. Though succinct, each volume is rich, and displays a balance between what Christians ought to value and what they ought to reject. This is one of the happiest publishing events in a long time."
—**William Edgar**, Professor of Apologetics, Westminster Theological Seminary

"When I was beginning my studies of theology and philosophy during the 1950s and '60s, I profited enormously from P&R's Modern Thinkers Series. Here were relatively short books on important philosophers and theologians such as Nietzsche, Dewey, Van Til, Barth, and Bultmann, by scholars of Reformed conviction such as Clark, Van Riessen, Ridderbos, Polman, and Zuidema. These books did not merely summarize the work of these thinkers; they were serious critical interactions. Today, P&R is resuming and updating the series, now called Great Thinkers. The new books, on people such as Aquinas, Hume, Nietzsche, Derrida, and Foucault, are written by scholars who are experts on these writers. As before, these books are short—around 100 pages. They set forth accurately the views of the thinkers under consideration, and they enter into constructive dialogue, governed by biblical and Reformed convictions. I look forward to the release of all the books being planned and to the good influence they will have on the next generation of philosophers and theologians."

—**John M. Frame**, Professor of Systematic Theology and Philosophy Emeritus, Reformed Theological Seminary, Orlando

G. W. F. HEGEL

GREAT THINKERS

A Series

Series Editor
Nathan D. Shannon

AVAILABLE IN THE GREAT THINKERS SERIES

Thomas Aquinas, by K. Scott Oliphint
Richard Dawkins, by Ransom Poythress
Jacques Derrida, by Christopher Watkin
Michel Foucault, by Christopher Watkin
G. W. F. Hegel, by Shao Kai Tseng
Karl Marx, by William D. Dennison

FORTHCOMING

Francis Bacon, by David C. Innes
Karl Barth, by Lane G. Tipton
David Hume, by James N. Anderson
Friedrich Nietzsche, by Carl R. Trueman
Karl Rahner, by Camden M. Bucey
Adam Smith, by Jan van Vliet

G. W. F. HEGEL

Shao Kai Tseng

P&R
PUBLISHING
P.O. BOX 817 • PHILLIPSBURG • NEW JERSEY 08865-0817

© 2018 by Shao Kai Tseng

All rights reserved. No part of this book may be reproduced, stored in a retrieval system, or transmitted in any form or by any means—electronic, mechanical, photocopy, recording, or otherwise—except for brief quotations for the purpose of review or comment, without the prior permission of the publisher, P&R Publishing Company, P.O. Box 817, Phillipsburg, New Jersey 08865–0817.

Scripture quotations are from The Holy Bible, English Standard Version, copyright © 2001 by Crossway, a publishing ministry of Good News Publishers. Used by permission. All rights reserved. All quotations are from the 2011 text edition of the ESV.

Italics within Scripture quotations indicate emphasis added.

ISBN: 978-1-62995-399-1 (pbk)
ISBN: 978-1-62995-400-4 (ePub)
ISBN: 978-1-62995-401-1 (Mobi)

Printed in the United States of America

Library of Congress Cataloging-in-Publication Data

Names: Tseng, Shao Kai, 1981- author.
Title: G.W.F. Hegel / Shao Kai Tseng.
Description: Phillipsburg, New Jersey : P&R Publishing Company, [2018] | Series: Great thinkers | Includes index.
Identifiers: LCCN 2018023137| ISBN 9781629953991 (pbk.) | ISBN 9781629954004 (epub) | ISBN 9781629954011 (mobi)
Subjects: LCSH: Hegel, Georg Wilhelm Friedrich, 1770-1831. | Hegel, Georg Wilhelm Friedrich, 1770-1831--Influence. | Reformed Church--Doctrines.
Classification: LCC B2948 .T74 2018 | DDC 193--dc23
LC record available at https://lccn.loc.gov/2018023137

In remembrance of *Yeye* and *Nainai*
who spoke God's Word to me and pointed me to Jesus Christ
who is the same yesterday and today and forever

Hebrews 13:7–8

CONTENTS

Series Introduction   ix
Foreword by Brant Bosserman   xi
Acknowledgments   xv

1. Why Hegel Matters Today   1
    Anecdote: From Hegel to Van Til and Vice Versa
    Hegel's Global Influence
    Hegel and Modern Theology
    Features of This Book

2. A Summary of Hegel's Thought   14
    Hegel's Thought in Context
    Hegel's Speculative Method
    Hegel's Dialectical Method
    Hegel's Philosophy of Religion
    Conclusion

3. A Reformed Assessment of Hegel's Thought   69
    What Reformed Thinkers Have Learned from Hegel
    Reformed Criticisms of Hegel
    Conclusion: A Christian Answer to Hegel

Glossary   129
Recommended Reading   149
Index of Scripture   155
Index of Subjects and Names   157

SERIES INTRODUCTION

Amid the rise and fall of nations and civilizations, the influence of a few great minds has been profound. Some of these remain relatively obscure, even as their thought shapes our world; others have become household names. As we engage our cultural and social contexts as ambassadors and witnesses for Christ, we must identify and test against the Word those thinkers who have so singularly formed the present age.

The Great Thinkers series is designed to meet the need for critically assessing the seminal thoughts of these thinkers. Great Thinkers hosts a colorful roster of authors analyzing primary source material against a background of historical contextual issues, and providing rich theological assessment and response from a Reformed perspective.

Each author was invited to meet a threefold goal, so that each Great Thinkers volume is, first, *academically informed*. The brevity of Great Thinkers volumes sets a premium on each author's command of the subject matter and on the secondary discussions that have shaped each thinker's influence. Our authors identify the most influential features of their thinkers' work and address them with precision and insight. Second, the series maintains a high standard of *biblical and theological faithfulness*. Each volume stands on an epistemic commitment to "the whole counsel of God" (Acts 20:27), and is thereby equipped for fruitful critical engagement. Finally, Great Thinkers texts are *accessible*, not burdened with jargon or unnecessarily difficult vocabulary. The goal is to inform and equip the reader as effectively as possible through clear writing, relevant analysis, and incisive, constructive critique. My hope is that this series will distinguish itself by striking with biblical faithfulness and the riches of the Reformed tradition at the central nerves of culture, cultural history, and intellectual heritage.

Bryce Craig, president of P&R Publishing, deserves hearty thanks for his initiative and encouragement in setting the series in motion and seeing it through. Many thanks as well to P&R's director of academic development, John Hughes, who has assumed, with cool efficiency, nearly every role on the production side of each volume. The Rev. Mark Moser carried much of the burden in the initial design of the series, acquisitions, and editing of the first several volumes. And the expert participation of Amanda Martin, P&R's editorial director, was essential at every turn. I have long admired P&R Publishing's commitment, steadfast now for over eighty-five years, to publishing excellent books promoting biblical understanding and cultural awareness, especially in the area of Christian apologetics. Sincere thanks to P&R, to these fine brothers and sisters, and to several others not mentioned here for the opportunity to serve as editor of the Great Thinkers series.

Nathan D. Shannon
Seoul, Korea

FOREWORD

Big achievements may appear in small productions. A dialectician the likes of Hegel knew this very well. An achievement as profound as absolute knowing could, he believed, be communicated in religious representations such as the Trinity and incarnation, as confessed by well-catechized children. In developing what is perhaps the most complex and all-encompassing system of modernity, Hegel made all things turn on these basic Christian ideas, even succinctly summarizing his philosophy with an allusion to Christ's call to take up the cross: *Die to live*.

Why should it be, then, that confessional Reformed theologians have found in Hegel an adversary rather than an ally? The simple answer is that Hegel's interpretation of these classic Christian doctrines is in virtually every instance heretical. But this answer raises a more profound question: Is it possible that a Christian reader of Hegel might at the same time be driven to a sort of admiration and bewilderment by engagement with this towering thinker? To the former, for his having assigned a more central role, for example, to the Trinity than many Christian theologies; to the latter, for his having missed the genuine significance of the orthodox doctrine so very errantly? And if so, how might one make positive use of Hegel's ideas without parting ways with Christian orthodoxy? In supplying significant answers to these sorts of questions, Alex Tseng's contribution to the Great Thinkers Series is itself a big achievement in a small production.

Not unlike Tseng, my interest in Hegel grew in conjunction with my study of the twentieth-century Reformed apologist Cornelius Van Til. Although he used Hegelian terms to describe his apologetic method, and gave passing summaries and critiques of Hegel's philosophy, I found myself frustrated that Van Til never provided a simple introduction to how he drew positive and negative inspiration from Hegel. Looking back, I believe a work like Tseng's would have significantly expedited my understanding of Van Til and his Reformed apologetic method. So I commend Tseng's volume to all those who would like to better understand an array of faithful Reformed theologians of the nineteenth and twentieth centuries.

But I would hate to imply that the lone benefit to Hegel study is the way that it may render *other* thinkers more accessible, and merely to academic students of theology at that. The truth is that since my graduate studies and academic writing, I have worked in the capacity of church planter and minister of Trinitas Presbyterian Church (PCA), and my appreciation for Hegel has not waned but grown. In preaching the redemptive-historical significance of Scripture, encouraging believers with the central truths of the gospel, and admonishing Christ's sheep to live by his commands and to rely on the ordinary means of grace, I have pondered again and again the idea that the substance of my ministry is not at all like a set of discrete propositions. The biblical stories, doctrines, commands, sacraments, prayerful petitions, and so on do not simply sit comfortably side by side or stacked one upon the other like building blocks. In ways too numerous to count and often difficult to perfectly describe, they fit together, work together, and grow out of one another—even when they may seem to conflict with one another. I feel a certain debt to Hegel for helping to sharpen my mind to reflect on the wonderful, surprising, and challenging connections within Christian truth.

And this state of affairs should not be wondered at. It is the Reformed theologian and pastor, after all, who believes that God has ordained all things to work together for his glory and for the good of his people. This confession commits us not only to reflect on how sin and tragedy will facilitate their opposite—the very glory of God—but to consider that a brilliant but tragically misguided thinker such as Hegel may have a positive hand in helping us to know and to love the living truth of our Savior. It is my sincere hope that this volume will lead many believers to appreciate Hegel in this fashion, even as they remain steadfast to a faithful Reformed confession.

Rev. Dr. Brant Bosserman
Minister, Trinitas Presbyterian Church
Mill Creek, Washington

ACKNOWLEDGMENTS

I would like to thank those who helped me in the process of writing this book. Nate Shannon has been a superb editor, not least because of his theological expertise. It has been a true delight working with John Hughes and the team at P&R Publishing. My buddy Nathaniel Gray Sutanto, always a source of theological inspiration for me, graciously nominated me for this project.

My reading of Hegel has been informed for the most part by my former mentors at Oxford: Professor Paul Fiddes, Professor George Pattison, Professor Joel Rasmussen, and Professor Johannes Zachhuber.

Daniel O'Connell and Peter Escalante kindly came to my aid when I needed research materials that were unavailable in China, where I wrote most of this book. Dan McDonald read through part of the manuscript and gave me helpful suggestions. My buddies Hong Liang and Thomas Coendet gave me authoritative literature on Hegel written in German to reassure me that I need not worry about possible criticism from Anglophone scholars who read Hegel in antitheological or antimetaphysical ways.

This book could not have been completed without the loving

support of my wife, Jasmine. I thank God for having enriched our married life with our dog Bobo, our lovely boy. He quietly kept me company in my study while I worked away on the manuscript, as if cheering me on, especially as I went through a somewhat emotional period.

My grandmother passed away during the composition of this book. She used to tell me bedside Bible stories when I was a boy. In the formative years of my childhood, both my parents went through an intellectual crisis of faith and temporarily stopped attending church. My grandparents were the ones who took me to church, prayed with me and for me, and "spoke the Word of God" to me. Now that they have both gone to be with the Lord—Christ desires to be with his people, as my friend Mark Jones loves to say—I would like to dedicate this book to them in remembrance of their spiritual leadership in my life as I continue to consider "the outcome of their way of life, and imitate their faith" (Heb. 13:7).

Soli Deo Gloria
Shanghai, China

1

WHY HEGEL MATTERS TODAY

Anecdote: From Hegel to Van Til and Vice Versa

During my freshman and sophomore years in college, I experienced an intellectual crisis of faith. God was still dear to my heart, as he always has been. Because no aspect of my life was of more fundamental importance than my very personal knowledge of God, I skipped many classes to visit the library, attempting to seek rational understanding of my own faith through philosophy. At that time, I attended a church in which most of the members, including the senior pastor, were intellectual elites from mainland China. The 1990s were a time when educated elites in communist or formerly communist countries began to give up faith in Marxism. Conversion to Christianity—be it theoretical, cultural, or personal—was a popular sort of "ideological turn to the right," so to speak, for many Chinese intellectuals. Most of our church members were evidently born-again Christians, but embracing Kant and Hegel appeared to many of them, at least at the initial stages of faith, to be an integral part of their ideological right turn, along with their conversion to Christianity. Under the influence of that cultural milieu, I decided to begin my philosophical quest with Kant and Hegel, picking up from the library *Groundwork of the Metaphysics of Morals* and the *Phenomenology of Spirit*.

I was, of course, puzzled by these works, primarily because of their difficulty. The vocabularies seemed esoteric; the arguments were too complex to follow. During my first reading of these texts, I developed only some very general impressions of these two Teutonic philosophers: Kant asserts that as long as we act morally, we do not need to know what God did for us, while Hegel contends that religion is intrinsically alienating as it separates human beings from absolute spirit, because of its necessarily "representational" form (we shall unfold this notion in chapter 2). These were, of course, vague impressions, and at that time I was not yet aware that all thinkers undergo intellectual development. Yet in retrospect I would say that these impressions were more or less correct, though perhaps not sufficiently precise or comprehensive. These philosophical views implied that I did not need to take the Bible literally as the Word of God, that I did not have to believe in the historical veracity of the death and resurrection of my Lord Jesus, and that while going to church would make me a better person, only by studying philosophy would I become consistently wise and good.

These were, of course, not the kind of answers that I was seeking, for truths such as the authority of the Bible and the historicity of the virgin birth were beyond doubt for me. My main problems as a sophomore student in physics in 2000–2001 were largely the success of naturalistic assumptions in the natural sciences (i.e., why would a scientific system that denies the workings of the hand of God in nature be so coherent and successful in explaining the physical world?) and the problem of evil (i.e., if God is good and almighty, why does he allow so much evil?). Walking away from Kant and Hegel with little gain (though, in fact, there was much to gain from them, if only I had been theologically and philosophically better equipped at the time), I devised my own theological explanations.

With much excitement, I presented this theology to my Campus Crusade leader, Dan MacDonald, a man of God who now serves as a Presbyterian (PCA) minister in Toronto. Dan told me that a long time ago someone named Pelagius had already come up with that theological explanation, and that it was deemed heretical. He invited me to walk with him to Regent College nearby, so that he could introduce to me the theology of John Calvin on our way. I was impressed by the theology he presented, so after we parted, I went to the Regent library and found a copy of Calvin's *Institutes*. Unlike my first encounter with Kant and Hegel, I understood the basic meaning of every sentence that Calvin wrote (though every time I revisited the *Institutes*, I would gain some new understandings). I finished my first reading of the *Institutes* almost in one breath, repeatedly shouting in my heart, "This man is explaining to me the God whom I have always known since I was a child!"

At that time, I thought I was done with Hegel for good. I began to acquaint myself with historic Reformed theologians, starting with the English Puritans of the seventeenth century, using J. I. Packer's introductory works. Eventually I made my way to modern Reformed theology, espoused variously by Old Princeton and Dutch neo-Calvinism. At that juncture, a friend who was studying at Westminster Theological Seminary in Philadelphia encouraged me to read Cornelius Van Til's *Defense of the Faith*.

Van Til gave me the confidence to engage in intellectual dialogue with non-Christian friends from the perspective of a Christian worldview. I picked up from Van Til an apologetic method that assumes the presuppositions of one's opponent's worldview, for argument's sake, in order to disclose their internal inconsistencies. In retrospect, I would say that my desire to debate with non-Christians in those days was driven more by youthful pride and audacity than by the glory of God in the proclamation of hope (1 Peter 3:15). Even so, the Van Tilian method proved to be immensely useful in practice.

Towards the end of my undergraduate studies, a Christian friend who knew me as an avid defender of the faith introduced me to a classmate from her church who was having serious doubts about Christianity. I tried to use Van Til's conceptual apparatuses to resolve his doubts as the three of us took the same bus home. Our conversation attracted the attention of a stranger on the bus who happened to be a philosophy student from our own university.

"Are you talking about Hegel?" the stranger asked.

"No, we're talking about Van Til," I replied.

"Who is Van Til?"

"A Christian theologian and philosopher."

"He sure sounds like Hegel."

At that time, my impression of Hegel was too vague to draw the connections, but I would soon find out that Van Til had actually been accused of corrupting Christian theology with Hegelian idealism in the 1940s and 1950s. Such accusations, launched by J. Oliver Buswell and others, were of course prejudiced, but they were not completely without reason. Van Til's doctoral dissertation at Princeton University was specifically directed against British idealism, of which Hegel was the patriarch, so to speak. Yet Van Til's opposition to Hegelian idealism was not at all simplistic. As Timothy McConnell puts it, "Idealism provided Van Til a framework for problems to be dealt with, and thus provides a reference for understanding his apologetical approach."[1]

As we proceed, we shall see more concretely how Van Til's apologetics—among other treasures of recent Reformed

---

1. Timothy McConnell, "The Influence of Idealism on the Apologetics of Cornelius Van Til," *Journal of the Evangelical Theological Society* 48 (2005): 558.

theology—is at once informed by the thought-form (*Denkform*) of Hegelian philosophy and opposed to the fundamental aspects of its ontology. Here Van Til serves as an example of how faithful Christian witness can benefit from critical appreciation of a philosophy that stands at odds with the presuppositions of biblical Christianity.

Hegel's Global Influence

Now the question is: in our own day and age, can we still benefit from a critical appreciation and charitable (though uncompromising) criticism of Hegel, like Van Til once did? There have been periods of time when Hegel's thought seemed to lose its contemporary relevance. The young Van Til lived in a time when British idealism was still a respected voice in the English-speaking world, and the influence of Hegel was felt within the culture. However, this philosophical movement, which began in the mid-nineteenth century, started to lose its cultural relevance in the early twentieth century. It faded into the background, with the rise of new philosophical traditions like analytic philosophy, existentialism, and logical positivism. Thus, McConnell suggests that Van Til's "usage of idealism . . . provides a potential limitation on the continuing applicability of certain aspects of . . . [his] apologetics."[2] The reason is that "by tailoring so much of his analysis to idealist philosophy, he lost his voice when his audience in the general culture changed to other forms of philosophy."[3]

However, history has shown us time and again that Hegel is one of those philosophers who keeps coming back, as it were, in different parts of the world in various circumstances. It is true

2. Ibid.
3. Ibid., 587.

that in the first few decades of the twentieth century, Hegelian thought and Hegel studies in continental Europe were briefly overshadowed by existentialism and postmodernism. Soon, however, philosophers began to realize that without a firm grasp of Hegel's system, it was impossible to truly understand twentieth-century European philosophers like Martin Heidegger, Jean-Paul Sartre, and Jacques Derrida.[4]

Another occasion for the revival of Hegelian philosophy and Hegel studies in the mid-twentieth century was the rise of communist regimes around the globe. Marxist philosophers in the Soviet Union and continental Europe were quick to acknowledge Karl Marx's intellectual indebtedness to so-called Left Hegelianism, which turned Hegel's idealism into a materialistic and atheistic system. Ernst Bloch and other Marxist philosophers of the twentieth century gave rise to renewed interests in Hegel, aimed at reinterpreting him as one of the fountainheads of dialectical materialism.[5]

Ironically, the eventful year 1989 in communist states around the world, which led to the dissolution of the Soviet Union in 1991, also spawned a new generation of Hegel scholars, both in the West and in countries like China. Western scholars of this generation tended to emphasize an *ad fontes* approach to Hegel's texts, allowing these texts to speak for themselves, without reading political agendas into them. In China, this new wave of academic interest in the German philosopher came with Deng Xiaoping's economic "reform and opening," which attempted to integrate right-wing ideologies of the West with Chinese communism. The events of 1989 meant for many Chinese intellectuals that Marxism had come to its dead end. Many of them

---

4. See Judith Butler, *Subjects of Desire: Hegelian Reflections in Twentieth-Century France* (New York: Columbia University Press, 1987).

5. See Guy Planty-Bonjour, *The Categories of Dialectical Materialism: Contemporary Soviet Ontology* (Dordrecht: Reidel, 1965).

went back to Hegel's texts to rediscover their implications for China's possible ideological turn to the right. So-called cultural Christians—scholars who appealed to Christianity as a way to reform Chinese culture without personal conversion—turned to Hegel, Kant, Max Weber, and others in their attempt to culturally "Christianize" Chinese society. It is worth mentioning here that the economic success of the "socialism with Chinese characteristics" program under the leaderships of Hu Jintao and Xi Jinping has led some of these scholars to "turn left" again and abandon the agenda of cultural Christianity. Others, however, gave up cultural Christianity to become born-again Christians, living as members of the visible body of Christ. As far as Hegel studies is concerned, China is starting to become a world leader in the Marxist camp of Hegel interpretation.[6]

The foregoing examples serve to demonstrate how multifaceted and sophisticated Hegel's philosophy is, such that it has been found deeply pertinent in so many different cultural-historical contexts. It is unlikely that it will become obsolete any time soon. For Christians and non-Christians alike, Hegel's writings will continue to be a source of both inspiration and challenge, in many different ways.

Hegel and Modern Theology

Another reason for Christians in particular to read Hegel has to do with his influence on modern theology, an area in which he stands as a towering figure. Virtually no major dogmatic theologian since the nineteenth century has been able to bypass him. The founder of modern liberal theology, Friedrich

6. This is reflected by the fact that the chapter on Marx and Hegel in *The Oxford Handbook of Hegel* is written by a home-grown Chinese scholar without education abroad. See Zhang Shuangli, "Marx and Hegel," in *The Oxford Handbook of Hegel*, ed. Dean Moyar (Oxford: Oxford University Press, 2017).

Schleiermacher (1768–1834), once Hegel's colleague at the University of Berlin, interacted intellectually with him at a profound level in a rather bitter rivalry.[7] Albrecht Ritschl (1822–89), next in line to Schleiermacher in the liberal tradition of modern theology, rejected Hegel's "speculative" metaphysics to embrace the "anti-metaphysical" approach of Immanuel Kant (1724–1804).[8] The ghost of Hegel's philosophy would continue to cast its shadow over the great anti-Hegelian Ritschlians, Wilhelm Herrmann (1846–1922) and Adolf von Harnack (1851–1930).[9] David Friedrich Strauss (1808–74), a pioneer in historical-critical studies of the Bible, who was once associated with the so-called Young Hegelians, introduced Hegelian methods into modern biblical scholarship (see chapter 3 of this book). This Hegelian influence has been there to stay in the discipline, even if many biblical scholars today are unaware of it.

In twentieth-century biblical scholarship, this Hegelian legacy was carried on by Rudolf Bultmann (1884–1976).[10] Karl Barth (1886–1968) is another twentieth-century theologian who was deeply indebted to Hegel, and the precise role of his influence on Barth's theology is an important ongoing debate in contemporary English-language Barth studies.[11] Among

---

7. See Shao Kai Tseng, "Church," in *The Oxford Handbook of Nineteenth-Century Christian Thought*, ed. J. Rasmussen, J. Wolfe, and J. Zachhuber (Oxford: Oxford University Press, 2017), 613–19.

8. See Joel Rasmussen, "The Transformation of Metaphysics," in *The Oxford Handbook of Nineteenth-Century Christian Thought*, 22–25.

9. Ibid., 24.

10. Bultmann's critique of and indebtedness to Hegel was a topic that drew considerable scholarly attention in the 1970s. See, for example, J. C. O'Neill, "Bultmann and Hegel," *Journal of Theological Studies* 2 (1970): 388–400; Kenley Dove, "Hegel and the Secularization Hypothesis," in *The Legacy of Hegel: Proceedings of the Marquette Hegel Symposium 1970* (The Hague: Martinus Nijhoff, 1973), 146–47.

11. I engage with this debate and offer a summary of it in Shao Kai Tseng, *Karl Barth's Infralapsarian Theology* (Downers Grove, IL: IVP Academic, 2016), 216–23, 227–30, 258–59, 273–81.

living theologians, Jürgen Moltmann (born 1926) is one of the luminaries most often compared with Hegel, not least because Moltmann sees God as needing the world as an other in order to realize himself as God, and sees the transience and sufferings of the world as having ultimately arisen from the inner nature of God. R. Scott Rodin puts it well when he comments that Moltmann contends "along Hegelian lines that the creation of another reality outside of Himself was the only thing God could do in acting according to His own nature."[12]

In conservative Reformed circles, the critical reception of the German philosopher in nineteenth-century Dutch Calvinism has been well documented (see chapter 3). Both Abraham Kuyper (1837–1920) and Herman Bavinck (1854–1921) were avid readers of Hegel. They were staunchly opposed to the contents of his philosophy, to be sure, but they also made positive use of Hegelian methods for Reformed theology. One of Bavinck's mentors in Leiden, Johannes Scholten (1811–85), even tried to incorporate Hegelian thought into the Reformed faith. In nineteenth-century America, Hegelian philosophy has also been an important lens through which Reformed theologians examined contemporary currents of thought and culture. The Old Princeton theologian Charles Hodge (1797–1878), for instance, analyzed the transcendentalist movement, influential in mid-nineteenth-century America, led by Ralph Waldo Emerson (1803–82), in light of Hegel's philosophy, criticizing the movement as "Hegelian to its core."[13]

Of course, I am personally acquainted with quite a considerable number of people within the Reformed world who might say, "But we don't care about modern theology," or "Reformed

---

12. R. Scott Rodin, *Evil and Theodicy in the Theology of Karl Barth* (New York: Peter Lang, 1997), 79.
13. Paul Gutjahr, *Charles Hodge: Guardian of American Orthodoxy* (Oxford: Oxford University Press, 2011), 233.

orthodoxy is all we need," or "Calvin and the Puritans are all we need." My friend Mark Jones says these things sometimes, but only jokingly for the sake of emphasizing the importance of Puritan theology and Reformed orthodoxy for contemporary Christianity. At a Hong Kong conference celebrating the five hundredth anniversary of the Reformation in the summer of 2017, where Mark and I were both keynote speakers, he emphatically reminded the Chinese Reformed audience of the breadth of reading that the Puritans exemplified: they drew from both Christian and non-Christian, orthodox and heterodox, sources.

We need not be reminded of Calvin's lengthy refutation of Osiander, in which Calvin actually recognizes the importance of some of the heretic's insights and his criticisms of the Lutheran doctrine of justification. The positive uses of Aristotle's philosophy in both Calvin and later Reformed orthodoxy is another example. Or how about Gisbertus Voetius's (1634–93) famous controversy with Descartes, and the more positive uses of Cartesian philosophy in the theology of Herman Witsius (1636–1708)? We could also mention Jonathan Edwards's (1703–58) critical appropriation of the empiricist terminology of the English philosopher John Locke (1632–1704), as well as his demonstrated familiarity with the writings of Thomas Hobbes (1588–1679), Isaac Newton (1643–1727), Joseph Addison (1672–1719), Joseph Butler (1692–1752), David Hume (1711–76), and many others.

Reformed theology in a vacuum is not historic Reformed theology. Historically, Reformed theology has always stood at the frontiers of culture, interacting with contemporary thought, be it theology, philosophy, or other disciplines. And because Hegel's influence has been so immense, profound, widespread, and multifaceted up to our own day, the importance of reading him cannot be overstated. Just the fact that Hegel's philosophy casts a shadow over modern theology should be sufficient reason for us to give him a read.

Features of This Book

Before proceeding to the main contents of this book, it would be helpful for the reader to understand the rationale behind the way I have structured the themes and materials I have chosen to cover. The basic motive is this: Hegel is very difficult to read, and I intend to try my best to make his writings manageable for the reader. After finishing this book, the reader should be able to approach Hegel's primary texts with confidence. To that end I have devised several features for the rest of the book, especially chapter 2:

1. Technical vocabularies defined: All the key terms of Hegel's technical writings and the relevant history of philosophy are highlighted with boldface letters in places of the text where succinct definitions are offered. These include terms like **rationalism, empiricism, transcendental idealism, absolute idealism,** and **speculative method**.
2. Historical overview: Hegel's philosophy focuses on the history of philosophy, and it is impossible to understand him without a basic knowledge of that history. At the beginning of chapter 2, I offer a brief account of the history of modern philosophy that finds its roots in classical Greece. This is meant to ensure that even readers who have little knowledge of the history of philosophy will be able to follow the rest of chapter 2.
3. Emphasis on method: Given the prescribed length of this book, it is impossible to cover all major areas of Hegel's philosophy in sufficient depth. Fortunately, Hegel is one of those philosophers whose method is said to be "identical" (we shall see what this means later) with his content. An outline of Hegel's philosophical method will give us

an understanding of the basic contours of his philosophy. This is intended to provide the reader with a map with which to steer through the convoluted material in Hegel's primary texts later, should the reader decide to pursue further studies of the philosopher's thought.
4. Analogies and metaphors: Hegel himself is fond of using lively and concrete metaphors and analogies to explain his rather difficult ideas. This book places an emphasis on this approach in order to make his philosophy more accessible to readers less familiar with the academic discipline.
5. Selective use of direct quotations from primary sources: A dilemma in writing an introductory volume on Hegel has to do with the use of primary sources. On the one hand, direct quotations are necessary in helping the reader gain a taste of the original Hegel. On the other hand, Hegel's writings are infamously hard to follow. The solution that this book has adopted is to limit direct quotations to those parts of Hegel's writings that are plain and relatively easy to read. In particular, quotations from the *Phenomenology* are taken from the translation by James Baillie (titled *The Phenomenology of Mind*). While this translation would not have been the choice for a work of scholarly research, the terms and phrases in this classic edition are dear to readers of Hegel, just as the King James Version is to English Bible readers. My hope is that through these direct quotations from Baillie's translation, the reader will come to feel the vibe of the English-language Hegel studies community, as it were.

As a last word before we proceed, let us remember that Hegel is a difficult writer with a style that is often unclear, and his works have been subjected to many different interpretations. It is true that his philosophy is antithetical to the biblical worldviews as understood by historic Reformed theology. However, we must also be careful not to misrepresent his thought. I shall try my best to offer an exegesis of his writings that is least controverted among Hegel scholars, even though it is inevitable that I will choose one interpretational model rather than another when it comes to certain issues. I am of the conviction that the most edifying way for Christians to engage with Hegel is one that is both critical and fair.

2

A SUMMARY OF HEGEL'S THOUGHT

Hegel's Thought in Context

The Philosophical-Historical Background

For a long time in the history of Western thought, theology, as the scientific study of God in relation to everything that is not God, has been central to philosophical discourses (here "science" refers generally to any discipline of knowledge that relies on defensible ways of knowing). For Plato, the task of theology is to speak of God scientifically in such a way that "God is always to be represented as he truly is."[1] Aristotle identifies theological knowledge as the summit of human wisdom.[2]

What to do with classical Greek philosophy and its methods has been a tricky business for Christianity in general and Reformed theology in particular. Yet it is hard to deny that the

---

1. Plato, *The Republic*, book 2, in Plato, *The Republic and Other Works*, trans. Benjamin Jowett (New York: Anchor, 1960), 56.
2. Aristotle, *Metaphysics*, book 11, part 7, ed. and trans. W. D. Ross (Oxford: Oxford University Press, 1979), 1064b5.

classical philosophers at least made it a normative conviction in mainstream Western philosophy that the *concept* of God is of paramount importance to all human knowledge. Many early Christian theologians adopted conceptual apparatuses and terminologies of (neo-)Platonism and Aristotelianism to communicate a Christian worldview to non-Christian philosophers in the public arena.[3] The rediscovery of Aristotle in Western Europe during the late Middle Ages made his **metaphysics** a dominant paradigm for approaching the big questions of philosophy—being and becoming, the purpose and meaning of existence, the nature and origin(s) of reality, etc.—which all hinge upon the very concept of God.

Although the humanistic impulses of the Renaissance (both secular and Christian) significantly transformed the landscape of Western thought and culture, philosophy continued to focus on a kind of metaphysics that has the concept of God as its foundation. This metaphysical tradition reached its heights in the works of early modern European philosophers such as Baruch Spinoza (1632–77) and Gottfried Wilhelm Leibniz (1646–1716). Of course, their accounts of God and the world lost the basically Christian characteristics of medieval scholasticism.

The modern rationalist tradition to which Spinoza and Leibniz belong can be traced back to the inception of the early modern period in philosophy. René Descartes (1596–1650), often dubbed the father of modern philosophy, introduced a way of knowing sometimes called methodological skepticism: he tentatively rejects all truth-claims on which doubts cannot be eliminated, in order to rebuild a system of knowledge on the basis of propositions that he thinks cannot be doubted. His famous statement, "I think, therefore I am" (*cogito ergo sum*), expresses what

---

3. Although many early Latin theologians, Augustine included, never read Aristotle, they were certainly under the influence of Aristotelian philosophy.

he thinks is beyond doubt. As far as epistemology is concerned, his philosophical point of reference is the knowing self rather than the revealed Word of God. When it comes to metaphysics, however, his entire system finds its basis in a so-called ontological proof of a benevolent God: because God, who created the world and endowed us with the gift of sensory perception, is good and does not deceive, we can trust that the world we perceive is real. Descartes's God, however, is the God of reason, rather than the living God of Scripture. In any case, the trademark of this school of modern **rationalism** is the presupposition that rational certainty about our thought processes provides the ground whereupon we can make sense of the external world.

On the other side of the English Channel, a school of philosophy known as empiricism began to gain prominence and rise against the rationalist tradition that dominated much of continental Europe during the early modern period. The forerunners and earlier proponents of empiricism, such as Francis Bacon (1561–1626), John Locke (1632–1704), and George Berkeley (1685–1753), just like the rationalists, were in fact deeply informed by Christian theology.

The central tenet of **empiricism** is that sensory experience is the primary or even the only source of human knowledge. This brand of philosophy found its most coherent and influential expression in the writings of the Scottish philosopher David Hume (1711–76). He boldly challenged the concept of causation that lies at the very foundation of traditional metaphysics. We can never be sure that there is such a thing as efficient causation, for it is beyond sensory perception. Hume came to the conclusion that traditional metaphysics, which presupposes innate rational constructs of the mind (such as the notion of causation) with which we can cognize and make sense of the world, does not render any true or certain knowledge of reality. Unlike his deeply theistic predecessors in the empiricist school, therefore, he rejected the possibility of metaphysical knowledge of God.

Upon reading Hume near the age of fifty, Immanuel Kant (1724–1804), on his own famous account, was awakened from his "dogmatic slumber." As Joel Rasmussen puts it, "Kant stands as the great watershed figure between the early modern metaphysics of Leibniz and the nineteenth-century system of metaphysics," represented by Fichte, Schelling, and Hegel.[4] Trained in the rationalist school of Descartes, Leibniz, and others, Kant's philosophical genius had been dormant for most of his life, for he thought that rationalism had sorted out all the important and basic questions of philosophy. He had been quite a prolific and renowned scholar during his early career, to be sure, but his works did not address the foundational problems of philosophy. Instead, he thought that he had inherited a basically finished system to which only fine details and minor planks were to be added.

All that was to change when Hume's empiricism sent Kant into self-imposed solitary confinement in his study. For eleven years, he did not publish a single work. The fruit was his epoch-making *Critique of Pure Reason* (1781), also called his First Critique. Craig Matarrese puts it well when he remarks that "Kant's project . . . should be considered as something of a last-ditch effort to save [the] Enlightenment self that started with Descartes: it was only with a drastically limited domain that reason could make good on its claims, and only with an elaborate set of 'postulations' that we could save morality and religion as we knew them."[5]

In an attempt to reconcile and integrate rationalism with

---

4. Joel Rasmussen, "The Transformation of Metaphysics," in *The Oxford Handbook of Nineteenth-Century Christian Thought*, ed. J. Rasmussen, J. Wolfe, and J. Zachhuber (Oxford: Oxford University Press, 2017), 12.

5. Craig Matarrese, *Starting with Hegel* (London: Continuum, 2010), 9.

Hume's empiricist insights, Kant proposes two distinctions in the judgments of human reason: (1) *a priori* as opposed to *a posteriori*, and (2) synthetic versus analytic. *A priori* judgments do not depend on experience, while *a posteriori* knowledge is derived empirically. Analytic judgments are those in which the subject already includes the predicate within itself (e.g., "all bachelors are men"). By contrast, synthetic judgments are those in which the predicate provides new information not contained in the definition of the subject.

The problem with empiricism is that it relies on synthetic *a posteriori* judgments as its primary way of reasoning, and this fails to produce any knowledge of necessary truths. By contrast, modern rationalism has traditionally been based upon analytic *a priori* judgments, but the result is a complex set of tautologies that lead to no new knowledge of reality.

Kant argues that only synthetic *a priori* judgments give rise to knowledge of new information that is necessarily true, and so they constitute the basis of true sciences (*Wissenschaften*). In other words, a truly scientific discipline must be based on synthetic *a priori* judgments. Arithmetic and geometry are obvious examples for Kant, while he goes to some length to show that the success of natural science (especially Newtonian physics) was also the result of its reliance upon synthetic *a priori* judgments. He then considers the possibility for metaphysics to be based upon such judgments.

Kant came to the same conclusion as Hume: he pronounced the unviability of traditional *rationalist* metaphysics, including what he called "rational theology." But here we must observe two important points. First, Kant's purpose was not to jettison metaphysics, but to restore its scientific status by giving it a new starting point that is neither simply rationalist nor simply empiricist. Second, his dismissal of rational theology was not an attempt to deny faith, but, as he puts it in the preface to the second edition of his First Critique, "to deny knowledge in order to make room for faith."[6]

The philosophical method and system with which he endeavored to accomplish these purposes is called **transcendental idealism**. These words may seem intimidating at first, but Kant's own definitions are not that complicated. First, an "idealist" is "someone who ... does not admit that it [the existence of external objects of sense] is cognized through immediate perception and infers from this that we can never be fully certain of their reality from any possible experience."[7]

One way to understand the term "transcendental" is that the possibility of sensory experience rests upon certain active categories of the mind. There are several schools of idealism, offering different accounts of how the cognizant self can cognize the world, and the term "transcendental" refers to the way "we cognize that and how certain representations ... are applied entirely *a priori*, or are possible."[8] Here the term "representation" refers to *the process by which a thing appears to us*, rather than what a thing is in itself (*an sich*). Transcendental idealism, then, is "the doctrine that they [all appearances] are all together to be regarded as mere representations and not as things in themselves, and accordingly that space and time are only sensible forms of our intuition, but not determinations given for themselves or conditions of objects as things in themselves."[9]

In other words, space and time are not real things in themselves, nor are they appearances of things that we intuit. Rather, they are the very form of our intuition: they are part and parcel of the mental process by which we cognize external objects as

---

6. Immanuel Kant, *Critique of Pure Reason*, ed. and trans. P. Guyer and A. Wood (Cambridge: Cambridge University Press, 1998), 117.
7. Ibid., 426.
8. Ibid., 196.
9. Ibid., 426.

they appear to us—not as they are in themselves. Because our sensory perception can only cognize objects in space and time, this form of intuition—an active process on the part of the cognizant subject—is a necessary precondition for external things to appear to us.

What this means is that we, as subjects of cognition, are not merely passive receivers of sensory data that is external to us. Our minds play an active organizing role in perceiving and understanding the appearances of objects external to us.

In the framework of this transcendental idealism, Kant states that as far as the theoretical use of reason is concerned, God, who transcends space and time, must be treated as merely a "regulative principle"—one by which the existence of a thing is posited for the purpose of facilitating the organization and interpretation of actual experiences.[10] Kant distinguishes between "regulative principles" and "constitutive principles": the latter claim the actual existence of things, whereas the former merely posit existence without making any metaphysical claims. Within the bounds of pure reason, he says, it is impossible to know anything about the existence of God as an object external to our minds.

This does not mean that Kant denies the objective existence of God, or that he sees God as only a postulate in our mental processes. In his *Critique of Practical Reason*, or the Second Critique, he argues that within the practical use of reason, ideas such as God "become immanent and constitutive inasmuch as they are grounds of the possibility of making real the necessary object of pure practical reason (the highest good)."[11] What this entails, however, is that religious faith is practical rather than rational: it

---

10. Ibid., 591.
11. Immanuel Kant, *Critique of Practical Reason*, ed. and trans. Mary Gregor (Cambridge: Cambridge University Press, 1997), 109. See John Hare, *The Moral Gap: Kantian Ethics, Human Limits, and God's Assistance* (Oxford: Oxford University Press, 1997).

is concerned with *doing* as opposed to *knowing*. In his dichotomy between faith and knowledge, he has effectively denied the scientific status of theology as a rational study of God.

In many ways, Kant's transcendental idealism can be seen as an attempt to rescue the rationalist project of making sense of the world on the basis of our knowledge of God in relation to the cognizant self and the self in relation to God. The net result, however, was a radically different approach to the fundamental questions of metaphysics, because Kant deemed these questions impossible to answer within the theoretical use of reason. This was practically a pronouncement that traditional metaphysics had come to an end, and so had rational theology.

The impact of Kant's transcendental idealism was immensely felt a generation later—in the generation of Hegel, which included the likes of Johann Gottlieb Fichte (1762–1814), Friedrich Schleiermacher (1768–1834), Johann Christian Friedrich Hölderlin (1770–1834), Friedrich Wilhelm Joseph von Schelling (1775–1854), and their earlier contemporary, Friedrich Schiller (1759–1805). Each in his own way, these writers labored in the shadow of Kant.

In what relation Hegel and other German idealists of his time stand to Kant has been a matter of intense debate. Fichte and the early Schelling are usually understood as having attempted to advance, correct, and complete Kant's project of transcendental idealism. The earliest writings of Hegel, too, show strong vestiges of Kantian thought. In these works (e.g., *The Life of Jesus* and *The Positivity of Christianity*), Hegel expresses deep concerns about the urgent need for a modern reinterpretation of Christianity. In the 1790s, "modern" basically meant "Kantian," especially for Hegel and his young contemporaries.

Yet even at this early stage of their careers, Hegel and Schelling were already troubled by certain aspects of Kant's transcendental idealism, not least his assertion of the unknowability of the thing-in-itself (*das Ding-an-sich*) as a result of what seemed to them to be an arbitrary severance of things in themselves (noumena) from their appearances or representations (phenomena). Equally disturbing to these two young, seminary-trained philosophers was Kant's pronouncement of the impossibility of rational knowledge of God.

In response to these difficulties in Kant's transcendental idealism, Hegel and Schelling would eventually devise a philosophical system known as **absolute idealism**. What sets absolute idealism apart from transcendental idealism is that the former no longer posits a reality-in-itself (*an sich*) apart from the mind. For absolute idealism, the mind is everything, and everything is the mind. The thrust of this approach to metaphysics is an identification of the cognizant subject (human consciousness) with its object of cognition (absolute spirit, which encompasses the whole of reality). The whole of world history is a process in which spirit actualizes itself through the total sum of human consciousness in each stage of history. This philosophy of ultimate (and, in Schelling's case, a more direct and simpler) identity between spirit and human consciousness was intended to overcome the noumena-phenomena gulf in Kant's transcendental idealism, thus safeguarding the possibility of rational knowledge of the world and of God.

As suggested above, however, how the idealism of Hegel's generation in general, and absolute idealism in particular, relate to Kant's transcendental idealism has been the subject of intense academic debate. In the specific case of Hegel, one mainstream view is to see him as reacting against Kant to recover the science of metaphysics as traditionally understood. On this view, the identification of God as absolute spirit lies at the very heart of Hegel's metaphysics. The mind of God expresses and realizes itself through the historical process of the development of the collective consciousness of his creatures. This means that we can come to know the ultimate reality of the mind of God through the philosophical study of the history of human consciousness. This interpretational model has been called "traditional metaphysical" or simply "traditionalist."

Another influential school of interpretation asserts that at the heart of Hegel's highly metaphysical philosophy is actually Kant's anti-metaphysical critique of reason. According to this interpretational model, Hegel's idealism can be seen as an "attempt to overcome Kant by means of Kant; not retreating behind him and seeking to go around him."[12] In more recent scholarship, some have carried the theme of the continuity between Hegel and Kant even further. The so-called "post-Kantian" interpreters have made the controversial claim that Hegel never taught the kind of traditionalistic metaphysics described above, and that he consistently subscribed to Kant's anti-metaphysical critique of reason throughout his career. On this view, Hegel's idealism is understood as an advancement of Kant's critical philosophy, registering corrections of Kant on the basis of his own critique, thus completing Kant's intellectual revolution by purifying it from the remaining vestiges of traditional metaphysics.[13]

These highly controversial assertions may seem extravagant to those familiar with Hegel's works, but they do carry some weighty arguments. The post-Kantian interpreters have at least called attention to the strong Kantian influences that can be discerned in Hegel's writings, thus forcing the traditionalist interpreters of Hegel to revise their views of him accordingly.

On a balanced reading, I think it is reasonable to acknowledge

---

12. Bruce McCormack, *Karl Barth's Critically Realistic Dialectical Theology* (Oxford: Oxford University Press, 1995), 465. Here I borrow McCormack's description of Barth, which is well suited for this interpretation of Hegel.

13. Representative of this school of interpretation are Robert Pippin, *Hegel's Idealism: The Satisfactions of Self-Consciousness* (Cambridge: Cambridge University Press, 1989), and Terry Pinkard, *Hegel's Naturalism: Mind, Nature, and the Final Ends of Life* (Oxford: Oxford University Press, 2012).

both the Kantian-critical aspect of Hegel's philosophical method and his textually evident attempts to rescue religion and traditional metaphysics.[14] This interpretation, often called the "revised metaphysical" or "critical metaphysical" view, helps us to identify Hegel's place in the history of philosophy in a more objective way by seeing him as a modern (i.e., post-Kantian) philosopher carrying forth the long metaphysical tradition handed down from his classical as well as early modern predecessors.

Many Christian readers who encounter Hegel's writings for the first time without preconceived interpretational frameworks would identify many strongly theological incentives in them. Just like his post-Kantian attempt to salvage the shipwreck of traditional metaphysics, Hegel's reinterpretation of Christianity at the heart of his absolute idealism can be seen as an attempt to secure a place for the ancient religion in modern society by construing it anew. Rasmussen puts it well: "Schelling and Hegel were the first to articulate a Trinitarian metaphysics in which the divine actually develops through the world of nature, history, and the human longing for transcendence. Their reconceptualization of God as dynamic Spirit in, with, and under the world, rather than as the perfect unchanging being fully transcendent to the world, signaled a radical modern alternative to classical theism."[15]

Hegel's Thought and Life: A Biographical Sketch

To better understand Hegel's theological incentives, it would be worth our while to briefly zoom in on his life. Born in 1770 in Stuttgart, Württemberg (presently part of the state of Baden-Württemberg, Germany), Hegel lived in a time of both intellectual and political uncertainties, and sometimes unrest. One common

---

14. One of the most notable representatives of this interpretational approach is Stephen Houlgate, *The Opening of Hegel's Logic: From Being to Infinite* (West Lafayette: Purdue University Press, 2005).

15. Rasmussen, "The Transformation of Metaphysics," 16.

myth about the spirit of his age—the so-called long nineteenth century—is that it was characterized by an optimism towards human nature and society, inherited from the Enlightenment ideal of the limitless powers of autonomous reason and evident in the social changes that secular humanism had brought about.

This is hardly an accurate picture of Hegel's time. The truth is that the French Revolution in 1789 led both to hope in liberty, fraternity, and equality and to fear of the cruelty and caprice of human nature now declared free from God. The Napoleonic Wars (1803–15) had left many parts of Europe in ruins, and Hegel witnessed the devastation firsthand—initially with deep admiration for Napoleon—when he was an unsalaried professor in Jena. In addition, the Industrial Revolution that began around 1760 had caused both hope and despair as it widened the poverty gap, creating a large low-income working class that would later come to be depicted in the early paintings of Vincent van Gogh (1853–90) and criticized in the writings of Karl Marx (1818–83). German nationalism began to take shape through the rise of romanticism in the poetry of Hölderlin and, later, the operas of Richard Wagner (1813–83). However, political turmoil in the Teutonic principalities and states cast a significant shadow over the hope for the unification of a "German Fatherland"—a "Germany above all in the world," which would "flourish in . . . radiance."[16]

The field of philosophy, as we have just seen, was also characterized by uncertainties. Young philosophers in Hegel's generation had realized that Kant's critical philosophy was tantamount to a death sentence to traditional speculative metaphysics, and many of them had gradually come to see that Kant's transcendental idealism was not a sufficiently viable alternative to answering the

---

16. These lyrics, written by the poet August Heinrich Hoffmann (1798–1874), were chosen as the German national anthem in 1922. After World War II, the national anthem was officially limited to the third stanza, and the "*über alles*" has been excluded ever since.

big questions of philosophy. The naïveté of Enlightenment optimism towards the limitless powers of autonomous human reason belonged to a bygone era. Reality-in-itself had been declared unknowable, and rational knowledge of God impossible. A new paradigm in philosophy was needed to supersede the old in order to account for the new *Zeitgeist*.

It was against such a cultural-historical background that Hegel began his studies in 1788 at the Tübinger Stift, the Protestant seminary affiliated with the University of Tübingen. There Hegel befriended his fellow student Schelling, and the two would eventually become the fountainhead of absolute idealism. That this form of German idealism should have arisen in Tübingen is by no means a coincidence. The religious atmosphere there was dominated by the mystical pietism of the German southwest. Compared to the Reformed heritage, this pietistic tradition does not tend to emphasize God's transcendence and the fixity of his special revelation. It encourages personal encounters with God and hearing his voice through devotions and mystical experiences, and so in this tradition God is seen as immanent in a way that (from the Reformed perspective) tends to compromise his transcendence. This provided a friendly environment for the philosophical study of humanistic Neoplatonism, of which Tübingen had traditionally been a bulwark. The thrust of Neoplatonism is that the whole universe is a hierarchical series of emanations from some form of divinity. Additionally, there was a revival of interest in Spinoza's monistic ontology in Germany. It is hardly a coincidence that Hegel and Schleiermacher, who both came under the influence of pietism during their student years, were among those who critically incorporated aspects of Spinozist monism into their own thinking. This panentheistic form of monism sees God as immanently dwelling within every individual substance in the universe, such that the universe as a whole is substantially divine. All these cultural and intellectual strands converged in

Tübingen to provide fertile soil for the kind of ultimate divine-human identity featuring prominently in the absolute idealism of Hegel and Schelling.

At Tübingen, Hegel developed close friendships with his two roommates, Schelling and Hölderlin. At this young age, they were enthusiastic supporters of the secular humanistic ideals of the French Revolution. It has to be noted, however, that in his early writings from the 1790s, Hegel already showed strong reservations about revolutionary ideals. Having witnessed the terror following the creation of the Revolutionary Tribunal in 1793, Hegel would come to believe that political hegemony and oppression cannot be extirpated through violence. If we can attribute a social movement model to Hegel's political philosophy, it would be moderate social reform. He would also agree to reactionary movements or even moderate resistance, but not revolutionary wars. Philosophy and religion—a kind of "people's religion" (*Volksreligion*), as a representation of philosophical reason—is for him the only way to establish true freedom in society.

Aside from their fascination with the French Revolution, the Tübingen trio also shared a keen interest in ancient Greek civilization. This was well in tune with the spirit of the age. Renaissance classicism had stirred up enthusiasm for Greco-Roman antiquity across Western Europe, but its depictions of the classical world were strongly biased towards Christian ideals. In the 1760s, a cultural movement called neoclassicism began to take shape in the visual arts, sweeping through Europe in the next few decades in music, literature, architecture, and other fields of cultural expression. Partly inspired by archaeological findings at newly excavated sites like Pompeii, the central incentive of the neoclassical movement was to rediscover the true cultural and aesthetic values of the classical world in its originality. Romanticism soon joined neoclassicism in celebrating the decadence of classical antiquity. Meanwhile, humanistic (both secular and Christian) interest in classical philosophy that originated in the Italian Renaissance had been deeply rooted in European culture for centuries, and, as mentioned above, Tübingen had a strong tradition of humanistic Neoplatonism.

Within this cultural milieu and under the influence of his friends, Hegel learned to cherish the classical heritage of Western civilization. Unlike Kant, Hegel was not so ready to give up the long-standing philosophical tradition founded by Plato and Aristotle. Some interpreters would go so far as to argue that Hegel was guilty of the uncritical mode of thinking that Kant had already proved to be obsolete. A more balanced picture would be to see Hegel as negating classical metaphysics with a post-Kantian critique in order to revive the speculative metaphysics handed down from the ancients in a modern form. This is evinced by Hegel's treatment of Aristotle in the *Lectures on the History of Philosophy*: Hegel is critical of the kind of "substance metaphysics" that Aristotle epitomizes, but he also finds in Aristotle's philosophy elements moving in the direction of a modern sort of "process metaphysics" (explanations of these terms—coined by later scholars—will follow).

The critical philosophy of Kant is yet another important dimension of the formative influences that Hegel encountered at Tübingen. Both his roommates, Hölderlin and Schelling, were avid readers of Kant and already preoccupied themselves with critical debates on the somewhat uncertain future of Kantian thought. At that time, Hegel was not nearly as interested in these debates as his roommates; his early writings from the 1790s show that he did not embrace Kant's critical philosophy until around 1800. Yet one should not dismiss the impact that these dormitory debates must have had on the young Hegel, who for a number of years to come would continue to follow the lead of his younger classmate Schelling. The friendship between Hegel and Schelling would eventually develop into an intellectual rivalry, and the two would sometimes criticize each other's writings with rather unfriendly mockeries.

Hegel completed his studies at the Tübinger Stift in 1793. He did not become a Protestant minister, as he had originally planned, partly because he had been disappointed by the corruption of the established churches and partly because, under Kantian influences, he had come to reject the dogmatic theology of historic Protestantism. From 1793 to 1801, Hegel served as a private house tutor, first in Bern and then in Frankfurt. His academic career did not begin until 1801, when he took up the post of an unsalaried lecturer at the University of Jena, where Schelling—five years his junior—was already an extraordinary professor. In due course, Hegel would come out on top in his rivalry with Schelling in terms of fame and influence, but during his early professional years he had to rely on Hölderlin and Schelling to secure his jobs in Frankfurt and Jena, respectively.

In 1805, Hegel was promoted to the position of extraordinary professor at Jena. The promotion was not offered to him. Rather, he had to resort to administrative maneuvers, seeking the help of none other than Johann Wolfgang von Goethe (1749–1832), who had served in various high-ranking capacities in the government of Weimar since the late 1770s. Still unsalaried after the promotion, Hegel eventually became financially destitute. Despite the hardship, however, he was still working hard to complete his first major work, *The Phenomenology of Spirit*.

In October 1806, Napoleon marched into Jena and, notwithstanding Hegel's express admiration for the emperor, whom he dubbed the epitome of the world-spirit of his era, he left the city and the university devastated. In 1807, Hegel was forced to leave Jena for his livelihood, taking up nonacademic jobs in Bamberg and Nuremberg. It was also in 1807 that he finally published his monumental *Phenomenology*.

He took up an appointment as headmaster of a *Gymnasium*

in Nuremberg in late 1808, which would last until 1816. During this period, his *Phenomenology* began to be read in German universities, which finally propelled his academic career to a delayed but smooth takeoff. In 1816, he received offers from the prestigious faculties of Berlin, Erlangen, and Heidelberg. Initially he chose Heidelberg, but stayed there for only two years before succeeding the late Johann Gottlieb Fichte (who died in 1814) in 1818 as the chair of philosophy at the recently established University of Berlin. It was while in Heidelberg, however, that Hegel published his *Encyclopedia of the Philosophical Sciences*, which many Hegel scholars today regard as his most definitive and significant opus.

The University of Berlin is the academic institution that Hegel is most commonly associated with, not least because he stayed there for over a decade until his death in 1831—the longest academic post he held in his life. The bitter rivalry with his colleague Schleiermacher, one of the founders of that renowned research university, who played a major role in excluding Hegel from the Berlin Academy of Sciences, has been a subject of scholarly interest up to our own day. The fascinating and intense debates between the leading philosopher and the leading theologian of early nineteenth-century Germany attracted a generation of young scholars to the new university, including the likes of Bruno Bauer (1809–82), Ludwig Feuerbach (1804–72), and David Strauss (1808–74).

While in Berlin, Hegel published a number of works that represent his most mature views. New editions of the *Encyclopedia* were published in 1827 and 1830. The *Philosophy of Right*, the most complete account of Hegel's political philosophy, was published in 1821. He also lectured on the philosophy of religion, the philosophy of history, the history of philosophy, and aesthetics several times during the Berlin years. Published posthumously, these lecture manuscripts and notes have also proved to be immensely significant for scholars who seek to understand the development of Hegel's thought and the maturation of his views.

In November 1831, Hegel passed away during a cholera outbreak in Berlin. He was already in poor health and it is uncertain whether he died from the epidemic or from the general deterioration of his health. Whatever the case, his legacy at Berlin would be passed down after his death for generations to come, exerting his influence in a wide variety of ways on some of the most prominent figures in German intellectual history— Karl Marx (1818–83), Friedrich Engels (1820–95), Wilhelm Dilthey (1833–1911), and Max Weber (1864–1920), among others. Needless to say, Hegel would also go down in history as one of the most influential philosophers of all time.

Hegel's Speculative Method

As suggested in the brief biography above, some aspects of Hegel's philosophy underwent important development during the course of his academic career. His philosophy of religion is an example that we shall treat in some detail in a later section. The philosophical method laid down in the *Phenomenology of Spirit* and explicated in the *Science of Logic* and the *Encyclopedia*, however, is a permanent aspect of Hegel's system, governing his thinking through all stages of his career from the early 1800s onward. In this section and the next, we shall examine two aspects of Hegel's method, namely the speculative and the dialectical. Note that these are not two different methods or separate parts of the same method. Rather, they are two descriptions of the same method as a whole: the speculative method is dialectical, and the dialectical method is speculative. But since these are distinct descriptions, it would help to consider them in separate sections.

In the *Science of Logic*, Hegel calls his method **"speculative."**[17] The term "speculative" has a number of connotations on top of its denotation. In a more general sense, it connotes the traditional type of "metaphysics" that has been "extirpated root and branch, and has vanished from the ranks of the sciences" as a result of "Kantian philosophy" that renounces all "speculative thought."[18] Here Hegel has in mind the speculative approach to metaphysics handed down from Plato and Aristotle to Descartes, Spinoza, and Leibniz. This tradition assumes that there is an intrinsic connection or correspondence between the mind and external reality in such a way that we can make sense of the world on the basis of rational speculation. This is evident especially in Aristotle's *Categories*, in which he contends that the categories of substance, quantity, quality, relation, place, time, etc. are intrinsic to the structure of the human mind, enabling us to cognize external objects. Kant's critical philosophy, as we have seen, declares that there is an unbridgeable gap between the human mind and external things in themselves.

One consequence of Kant's critique of reason is that theologians like Schleiermacher, who took this critical philosophy seriously, concluded that theology could no longer have God as the object of scientific inquiry. Schleiermacher tried to retain the scientific status of theology by treating it as a historical study of the church's dogmatic expressions of the essence of the Christian religion—the feeling (*Gefühl*) of absolute dependence on God.

For Hegel, this is far from satisfactory. He complains that

---

17. Georg Wilhelm Friedrich Hegel, *The Science of Logic*, ed. and trans. George di Giovanni (Cambridge: Cambridge University Press, 2010), 9. Matarrese offers a helpful summary at an introductory level in a section titled "Speculative Hermeneutics." See Matarrese, *Starting with Hegel*, 15–21. For a more advanced introduction, I recommend a chapter titled "The Speculative Method" in Murray Greene, *Hegel on the Soul* (Dordrecht: Springer, 1972), 23–37.

18. Hegel, *Science of Logic*, 7–8.

"theology, which in former times was the custodian of the speculative mysteries and of the albeit subordinate metaphysics, had relinquished this last science in exchange for feelings, popular practicality, and erudite historiography."[19] Instead of restoring the scientific status of the dogmatic theology of the church, however, Hegel maintains that God can still be a proper object of speculative metaphysical inquiry.

In one sense, therefore, the speculative character of Hegel's philosophical method suggests that it stands in line with the rationalist-idealist tradition of old, both classical and early modern. However, it would be a mistake to see Hegel as naively retreating to the old tradition in denial or avoidance of Kant's critique. Hegel's speculative method is distinctively modern and post-Kantian. As he puts it in the preface to the first edition of the *Encyclopedia*, his method is a "new reworking of philosophy" that he hopes will be recognized as "the only true method, identical with the content."[20]

Here Hegel breaks with Kant, on the one hand, and with the older speculative tradition, on the other. Kant's transcendental idealism, as we have seen, posits a gap between the *method* of knowing and the *content* of knowledge. In a different way, a sort of method-content separation is also posited in traditional speculative philosophy, evident in the ancient debate between the Stoics and the Peripatetics (followers of Aristotle) on the role of logic in philosophy. For the Stoics, logic is a proper object of scientific study, and the study of logic is therefore a proper branch of philosophy. The Peripatetics, by contrast, argued that logic, being an inherent construct of the rational mind, is only a tool for philosophical inquiry, rather than an object of study. In

19. Ibid., 8.
20. Georg Wilhelm Friedrich Hegel, *Encyclopedia of the Philosophical Sciences in Basic Outline, Part I: Science of Logic*, trans. and ed. Klaus Brinkmann and Daniel O. Dahlstrom (Cambridge: Cambridge University Press, 2010), 5.

the end, it was the Peripatetic approach that came to dominate mainstream philosophy down to medieval scholasticism and early modern metaphysics. As Hegel sees it, this separation of the method of philosophical inquiry from its content is a symptom of the ontological assumption that human consciousness is ultimately detached in one way or another from external objects. This assumption lies at the heart of Kant's transcendental idealism, which posits a gap between the rational mind and external things in themselves. Kant, as we have seen, concludes from this assumption that metaphysical knowledge of the noumenal world is impossible in the realm of pure reason.

Hegel's *speculative method*, then, is built on the metaphysical content of his philosophy—the ultimate identity between human consciousness and the external world as the manifestation of spirit in the process of history. According to Hegel's view of logic, the reason of human consciousness and the rationality of the world and its history are ultimately one, and this ultimate identity is the warrant for the scientific status of his speculative mode of inquiry into metaphysical reality. The task of Hegel's speculative methodology, then, is to uncover the essential rationality of the world that necessarily—rather than contingently—manifests itself through actual history, thus identifying the purpose and meaning of historical progress.

There are many ways to summarize Hegel's speculative method. In what follows, I will identify some key themes and notions in Hegel's project. The reader should bear in mind that this is intended only as an introduction that, given the complexity of Hegel's writings and the current state of Hegel studies, can be neither free of any interpretational framework nor comprehensive in its scope. The reader is encouraged to consult other secondary sources (see the appendix on "Recommended Reading") and Hegel's own works to gain a more comprehensive understanding of his philosophical method.

Concept and Representation: A Hermeneutic of the Concrete

An important distinction in Hegel's speculative method is that between **"concept"** (*Begriff*) and **"representation"** (*Vorstellung*). Representational thinking is a form of understanding associated with sensibility, while conceptual thinking seeks to grasp the rational essence of something. For Hegel, the rational is what is necessarily true and real; it is the "pure essentiality" of a thing. He does not deny the importance of *abstract* thinking and logic, but insists that the whole truth of this pure essentiality is knowable to us only as it actualizes itself in *concrete* historical reality. In actual historical concretion, however, a concept unavoidably takes on representational forms that possess contingent and accidental properties.

The task of the speculative method is to grasp the concept that lies behind its representations. The German word *Begriff* carries precisely such a connotation. It is derived from the verb *greifen*, which literally means "to grab or capture" something. The word *Vorstellung* is used in Kant's transcendental idealism to refer generally to the actual appearance of an object to a subject (i.e., actually intuited by the subject to become a concept and an idea in the subject's mind), a process that involves an active role on the part of the subject. Recall that for Kant, all that we can know is the representation of things and not things in themselves.

For Hegel, even though the representation of a concept unavoidably carries accidental and even contradictory qualities that veil the pure essentiality in itself, this does not mean that the conceptual rationality of a thing is ultimately unknowable to our consciousness. The knowability of the pure essentialities of the world to human consciousness hinges upon the relation between **consciousness** and **spirit**. In his preface to the first edition of the *Science of Logic*, Hegel sums up his view of consciousness in relation to spirit:

Consciousness is spirit as concrete, self-aware knowledge—to be sure, a knowledge bound to externality, but the progression of this subject matter, like the development of all natural and spiritual life, rests exclusively on the nature of the *pure essentialities* that constitute the content of the logic. Consciousness, as spirit which on the way of manifesting itself frees itself from its immediacy and external concretion, attains to the pure knowledge that takes these same pure essentialities for its subject matter as they are in and for themselves. They are pure thoughts, spirit that thinks its essence.[21]

These highly compact statements are difficult to understand, even for advanced students of philosophy, and I will try to unpack some key ideas here. It might be helpful to give a mundane illustration of how the speculative philosopher, as a conscious subject, can resort to "hermeneutical" (having to do with the science of interpretation) studies of external representations in order to gain conceptual understandings of the inherent rationality or pure essentiality of a thing.

Consider the game of basketball. I began watching basketball as a boy in Taiwan before I immigrated to Canada with my parents. It was the time when Michael Jordan and the Chicago Bulls had just begun to dominate the NBA. Like most basketball fans who started to watch the game at an early age, I had no one to teach me the **abstract** rules or the objectives of the sport. I simply watched the **concrete** games on television to grasp what the game is all about. The concrete *games* are the *representations* of the *game* of basketball; the *game* is the *concept* of the *games*.

In its representational form, basketball may be played at different levels—the NBA or elementary school teams. In the 1990s, nobody could have imagined how a player could sink

---

21. Hegel, *Science of Logic*, 10.

three-pointers like Stephen Curry. One might say that Curry is the epitome of the *concept* of three-point shots in a way that Hegel once thought that Napoleon was the embodiment of the spirit of his age. Yet both Curry and Napoleon are still merely *representations* of the essentialities that they respectively embody. Watching Curry in his MVP seasons of 2014–16, however, does give the fans a deeper comprehension of what the *concept* of three-pointers is all about. In this hermeneutical approach, the concept of three-pointers is not interpreted in terms of abstract propositions, but in terms of the concrete ways in which an actual embodiment of the concept—a particular basketball player—takes each shot.

The point of the foregoing illustration is this: the speculative philosopher seeks to grasp the *concept* of a thing by a hermeneutical study of its *representations*. For Hegel, it is impossible to grasp a concept truly without careful interpretation of its representations. The speculative method is one in which the philosopher starts with the particular and works his way up to the universal. This is the diametric opposite of modern rationalism and Kant's transcendental idealism, both of which proceed from abstract constructs of the mind (innate knowledge, innate ideas, space-time intuition, the categorical imperative, etc.) to the external and the concrete. To say that Hegel's idealism is *hermeneutical* in nature is to say that it seeks to understand the mind—human consciousness and spirit—by interpreting its concrete expressions in society, culture, and the history of philosophy.

Concept and Representation: The Teleological and Historicist Dimensions

Let us carry the basketball illustration further. A speculative philosopher starts out like a child who learns to appreciate basketball by watching the concrete games on television on her own. No one gave her a rulebook—she has to figure out the rules of the game on her own without the aid of "revelation." No one is there to teach the rules and objectives of the game to her, either—she is without the aid of "dogmatic authority." Perhaps by coincidence the first game she watches is one played by her classmates, who do not observe the rules strictly, and the referee consistently fails to blow the whistle for double dribbles. In this case, she encounters a rather poor representation of the game that does not help her to learn the rules well. Perhaps she would need to watch quite a number of NCAA games on television in order to understand all the rules pertinent to double dribbles and correct her misconceptions from the first game she has watched. Yet it is only by watching these concrete games, played well or poorly, that she can come to learn the rules of basketball.

Understanding all the rules (the normative aspect) of basketball is, of course, far from sufficiently grasping the very concept of the sport. To truly appreciate the game, one must consider its *teleology*—the philosophical study of purpose or purposiveness. Let us continue to consider the foregoing illustration. During the first game the girl ever watched, it should have been easy for her to understand that the most immediate purpose of the sport is to throw the ball into the basket. She would have learned that points are scored when this happens. By the end of the game, she would have come to understand that the purpose of a game is to score more points than the opposing team in order to win. As she begins to follow the NBA on television, she eventually learns that the purpose of the regular season is to win enough games to get into the playoffs, and the purpose of the playoffs is finally to win the championship.

For Hegel, the **rationality** of a concept necessarily carries a purpose or a series of purposes alongside its normative dimension, and this teleology is manifested through historical representations. Like the child who learns to appreciate the teleology of a sport by tracing the development of an NBA season, the task of the speculative philosopher is to identify the purposes of each stage of world history by investigating its development.

The purpose of basketball is, of course, far more than winning championships. Championships are merely a vehicle to motivate the players and teams to manifest the spirit of basketball in ever purer ways by elevating the game to ever higher levels. The Showtime Lakers, Michael Jordan's Bulls, and the Fantastic Four of the Warriors have all shown fans around the world aspects of the essential concept of basketball never represented before. Steve Nash's 2004–6 seasons have revealed a new dimension to the concept of a Most Valuable Player, determined by the magical passes and assists accomplished by his "Nash vision." Time and again in the history of basketball—not just the NBA—these "great men and women of history" have emerged to manifest to us various aspects of the very spirit of the sport by elevating it to new heights. To fully explore the teleology of the sport, it is essential to study its history and the great figures in it who are worthy of being considered embodiments of the very concept of basketball.

Similarly, world history comprises a series of bad and better representations of spirit that is to become absolute. The spirit of an age is best recognized in the "great men and women of history." A speculative philosopher can grasp the concept of the spirit only through close examinations of concrete historical representations. This emphasis on the investigation of history as purposive activity reflects the *historicist* dimension, or **historicism**, of Hegel's speculative method.

Process, Perspective, and Reconciliation

There is yet another dimension to Hegel's speculative method that can be explained by the basketball illustration. Imagine that after following twenty or so NBA seasons and playing in NCAA women's basketball herself, the child has now grown up and become a mother. Suppose that her son now plays for the same elementary school where she watched a basketball game for the first time in her life. The frame of mind with which she now watches the elementary school team play the sport is very different from her frame of mind when she first saw a basketball game in the same school gym. On the one hand, she has developed a *critical* mind, knowing how the game could be elevated to a higher level and how each player and perhaps the referee could perform better. On the other hand, as a mother, she is not indifferent to the way her son's team plays the game. Although she cannot enter the game herself, her consciousness is that of a participant in the game and not merely that of a spectator. What she sees, then, are not just the blunders and immaturity of the players. Rather, she sees potential in the team and in each player. The ultimate potential is of course the highest level at which the game could be played—a *pure concept* beyond the representations of even the Fantastic Four of the Golden State Warriors. This pure concept constitutes the *essentiality* and *rationality* behind the imperfect performances of the elementary school team; it is the force that drives each player and the team as a whole to develop into what they can *become*.

In this last illustration, there are three important points to note. First, according to Hegel, the *essence* of a thing is not *determined* (*bestimmt*) by what that thing *is* now—that is, the way the thing *appears* in its current form. Rather, the essence of a thing is what determines how the thing has *become* what it is at present, which is the same as what it can ultimately *become*. As we shall see in more detail, this is a revolutionary way of thinking about **being** and *becoming*. This is the thrust of Hegel's *process philosophy*.

Second, the consciousness of the speculative philosopher is akin to that of the mother in the analogy above. She is not indifferent; rather, her mind is very much in the game in such a way that all her criticisms, however objective and true, have the *perspective* of a *participant* and not that of a spectator. Just as the mother cannot go on the court, so also is it impossible for the speculative philosopher to go back in time and become a member of, say, Plato's Academy. Yet, as we study each stage of the history of philosophy and civilization, we should assume the perspective of an insider. Only then would we discover the *concept* lying behind the historical representations of the era and see what the spirit of that age is determined to *become*. If we were to critique a past stage of history as onlookers and outsiders, we would only criticize its faults and negate its value, without seeing what it had in it to become. More importantly, we would fail to see that the spirit of our own age developed into its present form only through a continuous series of historical stages in the past—not as different spirits, but as the same spirit in different representations.

Third, let us imagine that the mother is actually responsible for coaching the team. In this, she, as a speculative philosopher, is not merely looking at a past stage of history. Her son's team, as it actually is, here and now, is the stage of world history to which she also belongs—she is actually part of the team. If she is a good coach, she has developed a particular sort of attitude towards the aforementioned blunders and immaturity of the players and the team, the sort characterized by Hegel's notion of **reconciliation** (*Versöhnung*).

Reconciliation is of course a term derived from Christian theology, but in Hegel's usage it does not carry the kind of soteriological import that the biblical texts ascribe to it. The reason is that he does not think of the human plight of contradictions and transience in terms of the moral category of sin and fallenness. Humankind's alienation from God is not a result of some offence against him. Rather, God and humankind are ultimately identical as one spirit, and so this alienation is spirit's self-alienation. Spirit alienates itself from itself, in order to reconcile itself to itself.

Hegel's notion of reconciliation is primarily *ontological* and derivatively *ethical* in a sociopolitical sense. Ontological alienation manifests itself existentially in the problematic features of social reality, and the speculative philosopher must recognize that the human plight at present will eventually be sublated, or superseded (*aufgehoben*—explanations will follow later), by the process of reconciliation. Hegel himself puts it rather poetically in a famous line from his preface to the *Philosophy of Right*: "To recognize reason as the rose in the cross of the present and thereby to delight in the present—this rational insight is the *reconciliation* with actuality."[22]

To possess a reconciliatory frame of mind is to gaze upon reality and recognize *through* (and not just in spite of) its problematic representations what it has in it to become. In our basketball illustration, the coach possesses such a reconciliatory frame of mind, in that she sees potential in the team and in each player—not just in spite of, but within, their very failures.

Michael Hardimon's explanation of Hegel's notion of reconciliation is especially helpful here:

> Reconciliation, as Hegel understands it, is thus compatible with recognizing that the social world exhibits features that are genuinely problematic.... One cannot become genuinely reconciled by putting on rose-colored glasses; reconciliation is instead a matter of accepting the social world *as* a world that contains problems.... In Hegel's view, the delight that is internal to reconciliation must coexist with full appreciation of the suffering for which the cross stands. Consequently, reconciliation,

---

22. G. W. F. Hegel, *Elements of the Philosophy of Right*, ed. Allen W. Wood, trans. H. B. Nisbet (Cambridge: Cambridge University Press, 1991), 22.

as Hegel understands it, will inevitably be shadowed by a mood or feeling that could be characterized as melancholy.[23]

But if we return to the basketball illustration again, we should remember that the coach's reconciliatory attitude towards the problems of the team is by no means characterized by complacency or resignation. The coach's task is to identify the rose (the pure concept—the spirit of the *game*) in the cross (the problematic representations—the poorly played *games*), so that the team may be elevated to a higher level of performance that better manifests the essentiality of the rose. This is precisely the task of the speculative philosopher: to be reconciled with present actualities of suffering, injustice, oppression, and other forms of evil, with an active desire for progress, rather than for complacency or resignation, in order to elevate the world spirit to the next stage of its historical development, which will come closer to the rose that is in the cross of the present.

As a note of clarification, Hegel's notion of reconciliation is often described in terms of a "thesis-antithesis-synthesis" triad. This can sometimes be helpful, but it does not accurately convey Hegel's dialectics, or logic of mediation (see explanations in the next section, "Hegel's Dialectical Method"). It also needs to be emphasized that Hegel never used these terms; they were coined by Fichte. Hegel's dialectic may be better understood in terms of the logic of "the negation of a negation." This logic is deeply reflective of his background in German Protestant theology. We shall address its Trinitarian dimension in the next section, but here we can observe that this logic of mediation carries the basic thought-form of Martin Luther's theology of the cross (*theologia crucis*). The thrust of this theology is that the glory of

---

23. Michael Hardimon, *Hegel's Social Philosophy: A Project of Reconciliation* (Cambridge: Cambridge University Press, 1994), 90.

God is manifested through Christ's humiliation, which culminated in the crucifixion. Those who seek God's glory apart from the humiliation of the cross, says Luther, are unworthy of the title of theologians. There is for Luther an essential characteristic of double negation in the event of the crucifixion: the sin of humankind meets the wrath of God; death is sentenced to death by the death of Christ. Christ did not embrace the cross just in order to die, but rather to die in order to bring forth the glory of the resurrection. Yet it is only through the doubly negative character of the crucifixion that the glory of the resurrected life shines forth. Hegel's figure of the rose in the cross is strongly reminiscent of the German Protestant tradition of *theologia crucis*. The rose is by no means merely the synthesis of a thesis and an antithesis. Hegel's vision of reconciliation is such that the speculative philosopher, in Christlike manner, embraces the cross, not for the sake of the cross itself, but to bring out the rose in the cross through various processes of double negations. We shall return to this theme as we discuss Hegel's notion of "sublation" (*Aufhebung*) in the next section.

Much more could be said about Hegel's speculative method, especially how he applies it to his metaphysics and political philosophy. Due to the scope of this book, however, we are unable to cover all areas of his thought. His philosophy of right is one area that we regrettably have to leave out, but we shall examine his philosophy of religion in some detail and see how he treats religion as a representation of the concept of the absolute. For now, we turn to another overarching structure in the grand construct of Hegel's absolute idealism, namely, his dialectical method.

Hegel's Dialectical Method

The foregoing discussions have already alluded to the "dialectical" nature of Hegel's logic. As with the speculative dimension, dialectics is for Hegel a matter of both philosophical method and content. On his view, the historical process through which "spirit thinks its essence" by self-alienation and self-reconciliation is *ontologically* dialectical. This means, in simpler terms, that reality itself is by its very own nature dialectical. The dialectical method of philosophy is warranted by the very nature of its proper object: the totality of reality.

So what does the word "**dialectic**" mean in the first place? The word originated from a Greek verb that simply means "to converse with," which is also where the English word "dialogue" comes from. The Latin transliteration *dialectica* comes from a Greek term involving the word for "conversation" to refer to the philosophical art of debate. Dialectics, then, is simply a manner of philosophical investigation that seeks to uncover the truth through a process of debate between opposing voices. Plato's dialogues are classic examples of ancient Greek dialectics, which Hegel often acknowledges as the historical source of dialectical thinking. In these works, a certain character, often Socrates, serves as the voice of philosophical truth, unveiling the falsity or sophistry of the opposing voices of other characters through a series of questions.

Hegel's dialectical method is characteristically modern in that it challenges the *law of non-contradiction*, which Western philosophy had previously held to be axiomatic. This law, which can be traced back to Plato, dictates that two mutually contradictory propositions cannot both be true at the same time. The law of non-contradiction lies at the very foundation of Aristotelian logic. In his First Critique, Kant famously asserts that Aristotle has already written everything that there is to know about logic, and Kant also accepts the law of non-contradiction as an axiomatic criterion of truth.

On the basis of the law of non-contradiction, Kant argues against the scientific status of traditional metaphysics in his discussions of the "antinomies of pure reason" in the First Critique.

An antinomy is a case in which a thesis and its antithesis—two mutually contradictory statements—are both proved to be true by equally valid arguments or counterarguments. Kant shows that the traditional, speculative approach to metaphysical questions inevitably leads into the antinomies of pure reason that he identifies in the First Critique. This means, for Kant, that metaphysical truths cannot be attained speculatively.

Hegel does not really dispense with the law of non-contradiction (or the laws of identity and of the excluded middle, for that matter), yet he argues that the concept of truth is much more complex than can be accounted for by the traditional laws of logic. When we acknowledge the truth as the whole of a developmental process, says Hegel, we learn to come to terms with contradictions. One very helpful way to understand his dialectical method, then, is to see it as a presentation of the whole truth by the mediation of contradictions. The logic of mediation, as it is sometimes called, is the topic to which we now turn.

Truth and Mediation

The **logic of mediation** is a dialectical method that Hegel sets forth as early as his first major work, *The Phenomenology of Spirit*. It is explained in some detail in the preface—an admittedly unusual one, in which Hegel begins the work "by explaining the end the author had in mind, the circumstances which gave rise to the work, and the relation in which the writer takes it to stand to other treatises on the same subject, written by his predecessors or his contemporaries."[24] This preface is relatively easy to read, compared to the rest of the *Phenomenology*, and it would be helpful for the reader to read some direct quotations from the text as we go through this particular subsection.

---

24. G. W. F. Hegel, *The Phenomenology of Mind*, 2nd. ed., trans. J. B. Baillie (New York: Macmillan, 1931), 67. English translations of Hegel's *Phänomenologie des Geistes* (including that by Baillie) are often published today as *The Phenomenology of Spirit*.

Early on in the preface, Hegel warns that "the more the ordinary mind takes the opposition between true and false to be fixed, the more is it accustomed to expect either agreement or contradiction with a given philosophical system.... It does not conceive the diversity of philosophical systems as the progressive evolution of truth; rather, it sees only contradictions in that variety."[25] For Hegel, to take the law of non-contradiction as a universal criterion of truth is to misconstrue the very nature of *the* truth.

This does not mean that Hegel subscribes to a relativist view of truth. For Hegel, the truth is absolute. Better put, the truth is *the* **absolute**—in some translations and secondary literature, the first letter is capitalized to read "the Absolute." "Of the Absolute," however, "it must be said that it is essentially a result, that only at the end is it what it is in very truth; and just in that consists its nature, which is to be actual, subject, or self-becoming, self-development."[26]

Here Hegel is not merely challenging Aristotelian logic of old. He is getting to the heart of Aristotelian metaphysics, which he thinks is part and parcel of the logical tools with which it is constructed. Hegel's view of Aristotle is a controversial topic in the secondary literature, and this is closely related to the debate on Hegel's treatment of Kant—one with which we cannot engage within the scope of this book. Suffice it to say that although Hegel is known to have expressed profound admiration for Aristotle, even those who tend to identify strong continuities between the two thinkers would acknowledge that Hegel's program constitutes a paradigm shift from Aristotle's "**substance metaphysics**" to what has come to be called "**process philosophy**."[27]

25. Ibid., 68.
26. Ibid., 82.
27. The extent and nature of the German philosopher's continuities and disagreements with Aristotelian metaphysics is a debated issue. This is closely related to the previously mentioned post-Kantian controversy in Hegel studies. See Gilbert

Simply put, *substance metaphysics* is the view that the substance or substances constituting the whole of reality are a statically "abstract universality" characterized by "bare uniformity"—it is "undifferentiated, unmoved substantiality."[28] Hegel does not deny that the truth has such a substantial dimension, but this alone is not the whole truth. He understands the truth of reality as a historical *process* unfolding itself through dialectical stages.

In Hegel's view, "everything depends on grasping and expressing the ultimate truth not as Substance but as Subject as well."[29] This is to say that the truth of the universe is not merely an unchanging set of abstract forms, but also a living *subject* as well. Life is a process, and to say that the ultimate truth is a living subject is to say that it manifests itself through the process of its life. This means that even in its substantial dimension or "moment" (a term we shall explain later), the subject is not a dead, static, abstract substance, but *"living substance"*: it is "that being which is truly subject, or, what is the same thing, is truly realised and actual (*wirklich*) solely in the process of positing itself, or in mediating with its own self its transitions from one state or position to the opposite."[30] In other words, "true reality ... is the process of its own becoming, the circle which presupposes its end or its purpose, and has its end for its beginning; it becomes concrete and actual only by being carried out, and by the end it involves."[31]

In this process of becoming, the all-encompassing truth of

Gérard, "Hegel, lecteur de la métaphysique d'Aristote. La substance en tant que sujet," *Revue de Métaphysique et de Morale* 74 (2012): 195–223; Nicholas Lobkowicz, "Substance and Reflection: Hegel and Aristotle," *Review of Metaphysics* 43 (1989): 27–46; Béatrice Longuenesse, *Hegel's Critique of Metaphysics* (Cambridge: Cambridge University Press, 2007).

28. Hegel, *Phenomenology*, 80.
29. Ibid.
30. Ibid.
31. Ibid., 81.

the universe undergoes *self-differentiation, self-alienation, self-objectification*, and therefore inevitable *self-contradiction*. This, however, is only a second dimension or stage of the whole truth. The whole truth is a process of *mediation*. Hegel contrasts **mediation** with **immediacy**. Immediacy is the stage in which truth is expressed merely as abstract universals. It is the moment in which spirit is only *in itself* (*an sich*), but without itself as a differentiated object. The process of self-objectification, represented by the Trinitarian doctrine of the eternal generation of the Son, allows spirit to be *for itself* (*für sich*). But in this second moment, spirit becomes an *other* (*Anderssein*) to itself, which contradicts its very own simplicity. A third moment is thus necessary to complete the process of the development of the whole truth—the process of mediation. This moment is represented by the Trinitarian doctrine of the procession of the Holy Spirit, which allows spirit to be both *in and for itself* (*an und für sich*), and thus to be what it is essentially—the absolute.

The doctrine of the Trinity, as Hegel sees it, is "the idea which represents the Absolute as Spirit (*Geist*)—the grandest conception of all."[32] **The absolute** as **spirit** is not just the essence of reality. Spirit is the sum of all reality: "Spirit is alone Reality."[33] The absolute is spirit fully actualized *qua* spirit through the process of mediation, the objective-subjective-absolute triad. The process of mediation that spirit undergoes constitutes the whole of reality, and *the truth* is the whole of this process. One must embrace contradictions if one wishes to grasp the whole truth. "The truth is the whole. The whole, however, is merely the essential nature reaching its completeness through the process of its own development."[34] This ontological understanding of the truth as a process dictates the *dialectical* nature of Hegel's

32. Ibid., 85.
33. Ibid., 86.
34. Ibid., 81.

method. He consistently applies the logic of mediation set forth at the beginning of the *Phenomenology* to his interpretations of the progress of world history in his later works.

Organicism: The Dialectic of Cultivation (*Bildung*)

The foregoing discussions of Hegel's understanding of the truth as a "whole," a "living substance," a subject that lives through the process of its life, have already alluded to the *organicist* dimension of Hegel's dialectics. **Organicism**, simply stated, refers generally to the kind of philosophy that treats reality and the truths concerning reality as an organic whole, akin to a living organism, whose constituent parts are biologically interrelated in such a way that together they sustain the life of the organism and contribute to its growth. Understood organically, propositional truths are valid, not as abstract propositions that are true in themselves, but as truthful predications about reality likened in one way or another to a living subject. Organicism is characterized by the use of *organic metaphors* as a key to interpreting reality and the truths concerning it.

An example familiar to Christian readers would be the way in which the apostle Paul describes Christ and the church as the head and the body, and the church as a living body with different members carrying out different functions. This organic metaphor helps us to understand the descriptive and prescriptive propositions regarding Christ and the church as the *living* truth of God in relation to his people, rather than as abstract truths that are valid in themselves apart from God and his will. Paul's statement of Christ's universal lordship as the head of the church, for example, is a truthful predication of living relations between Christ, his people, and his creation (Eph. 1:23). The divine image of diversity in unity manifested through the church, of which neo-Calvinist theologians are fond to speak, is also described in terms of the aforementioned organic metaphor (Eph. 4:4–6, 11–13, 15–16).

The prescriptive propositions regarding headship and sacrifice are not "categorical imperatives" of a Kantian sort, but rather the will of the living God for the organic relations between Christ and the church, and, by analogy, between husband and wife (Eph. 5:21–33).

Hegel's organicism is a frequently discussed topic in the secondary literature. Reformed theologians of the neo-Calvinist tradition often borrow Hegel's organicist themes in critical ways, sometimes for polemical purposes. James Eglinton has observed that both Hegel and Bavinck "attempt to be rigorously organic in style and substance," and that understanding Bavinck's conscious commitment to organicism is important for appreciating his critique of Hegelian idealism.[35] In chapter 3 of this book, we shall rely on Bavinck to offer a Reformed assessment of Hegel's thought, and return to the topic of their respective uses of organic motifs.

For now, we shall focus on Hegel. His organicist thinking is often compared to modern rationalist tendencies to dissect truth and reality analytically in order to examine the constituent parts individually. This way of thinking fails to recognize the truth of the universe as a living subject. While Aristotle is largely responsible for the tendency towards what we described earlier as "substance metaphysics" in the history of Western philosophy, Hegel also acknowledges Aristotle as the source of the organicist way of thinking characteristic of process philosophy. He writes that in the sense in which Aristotle "characterises nature as purposive activity, purpose is the immediate, the undisturbed, the unmoved which is self-moving; as such it is subject."[36] Even so, however, the understanding of substance as a living subject is, at best, latent in Aristotle's writings. For the most part in the history

---

35. James Eglinton, *Trinity and Organism: Towards a New Reading of Herman Bavinck's Organic Motif* (London: T&T Clark, 2012), 66.

36. Hegel, *Phenomenology*, 83.

of Western philosophy, metaphysics has manifested a strong tendency towards substantialist ways of thinking that are inorganic.

The Hegelian distinction between substance metaphysics and process metaphysics can be understood in the following way. While "substance metaphysics" is not a term Hegel himself uses, it is derived from his consistent reference to the category of substance in his interpretation of the general characteristics of mainline philosophy since Plato and Aristotle, which he famously dubbed a "tendency towards substance."[37] In the *Encyclopedia of Logic*, for instance, he criticizes Spinoza for treating God "only as *substance* and not as subject and spirit."[38] Here Hegel has in mind a kind of lifeless, mindless, static substance, which he contrasts to a living *subject*. As explained earlier, a living subject does possess a substantial dimension, or "moment," but even in this moment it is a "living substance" undergoing a process of organic development.

One of the most significant differences between substantialist and process ways of thinking lies in the following. Substance metaphysics sees the nature of reality as static. In Aristotelian terms, "nature" is the "potentiality" of a thing that dictates what it is to become in "actuality." In other words, the actuality of a thing is determined by the potentiality of its nature: becoming is determined by being. Hegel, by contrast, contends that what a thing *is* at present is determined by what it has in it to *become*: being is determined by becoming.

These rather difficult and abstract statements are easily understood in light of Hegel's organic metaphors. Consider the example of a human embryo.[39] The embryonic stage is certainly

---

37. See Johanna Seibt, "Particulars," in *Theory and Applications of Ontology: Philosophical Perspectives*, ed. Johanna Seibt and Roberto Poli (New York: Springer, 2010), 28.

38. G. W. F. Hegel, *The Encyclopaedia Logic*, trans. T. F. Geraets, W. A. Suchting, and H. S. Harris (Indianapolis, IN: Hackett Publishing Company, 1991), 8.

39. Hegel, *Phenomenology*, 83.

a part of the process of the life of a human being. Yet "in itself" (*an sich*) it is only "implicitly a human being" in the sense that it has not yet "by itself" (*für sich*, better translated as "for itself") gone through the life process that constitutes the whole living nature of humanity.[40]

The more conventional, substantialist way of seeing this picture would be to think that a static "human nature"—the form of a human being that sets the human race apart from other things—constitutes the human substance, which determines what the embryo is to become. While this understanding is not wrong, Hegel thinks that it fails to capture the bigger picture, that is, to see "nature" and "substance" as "process" or "living substance."

In the case of the embryo, Hegel says that rather than seeing its development as having been determined by what it statically is as a human substance, the bigger picture would be to see what it is in its present form (*Gestalt*) as having been determined by what it has in it to become. In other words, it is the whole process of human life that determines its being as an embryo at the present stage. It is the human being "in the form of *developed* and *cultivated* reason" that has "made itself to be what it is implicitly" in its embryonic form.[41]

Here Hegel refers to the notion of **cultivation** (*Bildung*), an overarching theme in his writings. The German word comes from the noun *das Bild*, which means "picture" or "image." In its modern usage, *Bildung* usually refers to "education" in the broader sense of inculcation and social formation, and not just institutional schooling (*Erziehung*). The interesting association between "image" and "education" has its roots in medieval German mysticism, in which believers were taught to meditate on religious images for the purpose of spiritual formation. In the long nineteenth century, the

40. Ibid.
41. Ibid.

notion of *Bildung* became a core value of German culture. The literary tradition of *Bildungsroman* (a word compounded from *Bildung* and *Roman*, the German word for "novel"), associated with but not restricted to German romanticism, thrived during this period. Works of this genre, such as Goethe's *Wilhelm Meister's Apprenticeship* (1795–96), are characterized by their thematic focus on the protagonist's mental growth and personal formation. Pastors and theologians like Schleiermacher came to see one of their chief tasks as bringing Christianity to the cultured—the *Gebildete* (from *bilden*, the verbal form of *Bildung*)—by convincing them that religion is indispensable for the process of *Bildung*. This was precisely his aim in his famous early title, *On Religion: Speeches to Its Cultured Despisers* (*Über die Religion: Reden an die Gebildeten unter ihren Verächtern*).

Hegel applies the notion of *Bildung* to both personal cultivation and the developmental progress of spirit through the process of world history. The process of cultivation begins with "the struggle to pass out of the unbroken immediacy of naïve psychical life."[42] What Hegel means here can be likened to a child passing from infancy to the next stage of life, in which he begins to acquire knowledge consciously. At this stage, the kind of knowledge that he struggles to acquire is that of "universal principles."[43] This is analogous to the collective consciousness of human society in classical antiquity. "This beginning of mental cultivation will, however, very soon make way for the earnestness of actual life in all its fullness, which leads to a living experience of the subject-matter itself."[44]

Taken as a whole, the history of the cultivation of spirit is a process in which collective human consciousness passes from *representational* understanding (*Vorstellung*) to *conceptual*

42. Ibid., 70.
43. Ibid.
44. Ibid.

understanding (*Begriff*) of the whole of reality, which is none other than spirit itself. In both the case of a human individual and that of spirit, cultivation involves a painful process of self-alienation, in which it seeks to understand and recognize (*anerkennen*) itself as an objective other, followed by a process of self-reconciliation, through which it finally realizes itself as both *in* itself and *for* itself. That is to say, human consciousness finally comes to understand that the objective reality it seeks to grasp is none other than itself as a particular and concrete manifestation of spirit.

Hegel describes the process of cultivation as being gradual, for the most part. In the course of history, however, great men like Plato (and himself) would appear at the crucial junctures of cultural development to take the collective consciousness of human society to the next stage. The development from one stage to the next is not smooth or gradual, but involves a qualitative leap. This leap in the process of growth must again be understood organically:

> It [spirit] is indeed never at rest, but carried along the stream of progress ever onward. But it is here as in the case of the birth of a child; after a long period of nutrition in silence, the continuity of the gradual growth in size, of quantitative change, is suddenly cut short by the first breath drawn—there is a break in the process, a qualitative change—and the child is born. In like manner the spirit of the time, growing slowly and quietly ripe for the new form it is to assume, disintegrates one fragment after another of the structure of its previous world.[45]

The driving force of this process is spirit's desire for conceptual understanding of the *whole* truth. Hegel uses the organic metaphor of plant growth to explain this: "When we want to

45. Ibid., 75.

see an oak with all its vigour of trunk, its spreading branches, and mass of foliage, we are not satisfied to be shown an acorn instead."[46] This painful sense of dissatisfaction is characteristic of the process of cultivation. The growing pains, as it were, propel spirit to advance in the dialectical development of its own history. These pains are reflected in the actual sufferings and conflicts of the world, but again, in order to grow to maturation and see the rose, we must embrace the cross of the present. Only then will spirit realize itself in the thinking of its own essence and attain to the essentiality of its freedom expressed in actual human society.

The Three Moments of Logic: The Dialectic of Sublation (*Aufhebung*)

The logic of Hegel's dialectical method finds its most succinct and systematic statement in the first part of the *Encyclopedia of Philosophical Sciences*, which deals with the science of logic. A summary of the "precise conception and division of the logic," in the form of a three-moment dialectic, is set forth in §§79–82.[47] The style of writing here is much more technical than the preface to the *Phenomenology*, and so I will refrain from quoting directly from the text except when necessary or helpful (that is, in cases where Hegel himself resorts to everyday language to make things clear for his reader).

At the beginning of §79, Hegel states that "with regard to its form, the *logical* has three sides."[48] These are (1) "*the side of abstraction* or *of the understanding*," (2) "*the dialectical* or *negatively rational side*," and (3) "*the speculative* or *positively rational* one."[49] The reader can be reassured here that these terms are not nearly as difficult as they are intimidating.

46. Ibid., 76.
47. Hegel, *The Encyclopaedia Logic*, 125.
48. Ibid. Italics original.
49. Ibid. Italics original.

Before moving on to explain each side of the dialectic, Hegel explains that these are not three "parts," but rather three "**moments**" of "the Logic," which he defines as "*everything logically real*," that is, "every concept or . . . everything true in general."[50] The word "moment" here is a direct translation of the German word *Moment*, the denotations of which are broader than its English equivalent. *Moment* can refer to a moment in time, but it can also designate an "element" or "factor." Hegel's usage carries all these significations. The three moments are *elements* of the same reality, but not as parts of the whole; rather, each moment *is* the whole of the same reality in a different dimension than the other two. Here Hegel is applying Trinitarian patterns of thinking to his understanding of logic as the whole of reality. According to the Christian doctrine of the Trinity, the three persons of the one Godhead are not three parts of it; rather, each distinct person possesses the fullness of God's being.

Unlike the coeternity of the three persons of God, however, Hegel's logical trinity consists in the temporal process of successive moments developed through the course of history. Let us note again that this dialectical logic conveys both the *method* and the *content* of Hegel's philosophy. It is a way of thinking that reflects the nature of reality *qua* spirit, which realizes itself through the dialectical process of history. The three-moment dialectic not only characterizes this entire process as a whole, but also all its details and aspects considered individually.

In the first moment, which is that "*of abstraction* or *of the understanding*," the human mind conceives of the external world in terms of universal forms, which Aristotle calls secondary substances or natures. Early Christian thinkers resorted to the biblical phrase "according to their kinds" (Gen. 1:20–24) for this basically Platonic understanding of substances. Intuitively,

---

50. Ibid. Italics original.

this way of thinking makes a lot of sense. For instance, once a child has learned what the abstract idea of a cat is, his parents would not need to explain to him, every time he sees a cat, *that* and *how* this animal is a cat. He has abstracted from the limited number of *particular* cats that he has seen the *universal form* of cats. In this moment of logic, such universal forms are understood to be the static natures and definitions of different kinds of things. That is, *substance* has not yet come to be appreciated as living *subject*. Note that this moment of abstract understanding, just like the two following moments, pertains both to the subjective understanding of human consciousness and to the objective reality of the world, which, as we have seen, are ultimately one.

Here it would be helpful for us to mention that while Hegel still retains the vocabulary of traditional substance metaphysics to describe the first moment of logic (words such as "substance," "essence," and "nature"), he resorts to a neologism to better convey the "true" concept of these words. The technical term is **determination** (*Bestimmung*). The full meaning of this Hegelian term is quite complex. It can be understood as a dialectical notion with which Hegel replaces or fleshes out the more statically substantialist conception of nature or essence. Stephen Houlgate describes "determination" in relational terms as "the specific quality or character that something manifests or asserts in its relation to an other."[51] A more historicist nuance is expressed in Terje Sparby's explanation of the notion as "the uncovering of the essential nature of something" through the dialectical process of history.[52] In an otherwise somewhat oversimplified way, we might understand "determination" as the *definition* of a substance understood in Hegelian terms as living subject.

---

51. Stephen Houlgate, *The Opening of Hegel's Logic: From Being to Infinity* (West Lafayette, IN: Purdue University Press, 2006), 348.

52. Terje Sparby, *Hegel's Conception of the Determinate Negation* (Leiden: Brill, 2015), 200.

In the second moment of logic, the ostensibly static determination of the previous moment evolves into its opposite. This second moment, which Hegel calls "*the dialectical* or *negatively rational,*" is thus characterized by contradictions and uncertainties. This process is explicated in light of another important technical Hegelian term: **sublation** (*Aufhebung*). This term is sometimes translated as "supersession," which does convey the meaning quite well, but loses the idiosyncrasy of Hegel's use of the word *Aufhebung* in German. The German verb *heben* means "to lift," and *aufheben* in its ordinary usage can mean either "to cancel/abrogate" or "to lift up/elevate." Hegel combines both denotations of *aufheben* to refer to the abrogation or negation of a previous moment, not for the purpose of annihilating it, but rather to elevate it to the next, positive moment. On this view, "sublation" in its narrower sense refers to the second, negative moment of logic, namely, the negation of the previous moment. In its broader sense, however, the three-moment dialectic as a whole can be described as a process of sublation.

Earlier we mentioned that sometimes the logic of "sublation" is described as "the negation of a negation." If the foregoing explanation sounds as idiosyncratic as the term itself, we can resort to the organic metaphor of metamorphosis for pedagogical purposes, although Hegel himself cautions that this analogy has its shortcomings, for it describes the dialectical progress only of an individual and not of a genus.[53] Even then, however, I find the metamorphosis metaphor to be among the most helpful in explaining the dialectic of sublation. In the first moment of its metamorphosis, the insect carries the form of a caterpillar, which is not particularly appealing in appearance. This form is negated or sublated by the second moment in the form of a pupa.

53. G. W. F. Hegel, *Hegel's Philosophy of Nature: Part Two of the* Encyclopaedia of the Philosophical Sciences (1830), trans. A. V. Miller (New York: Oxford University Press, 2004), 22.

The pupa, however, is not the final purpose of the sublation. It is only tentative, carrying the dialectical nature of contradictions. It serves to elevate the same subject to its third moment—the beautiful butterfly.

This third moment of logic is *"the speculative* or *positively rational."* It is the *reconciliation* of the previous contradiction, the *mediation* of the opposites, resulting in their unity. The tentative negation of the previous moment is now elevated to the moment of positive reason. In this last moment, the truth as a whole is comprehended in terms of the process of its development as a subject.

Hegel applies this three-moment dialectic to every aspect of his philosophy. The most well known is perhaps his *trinity* of being, which he construes as the triad of *being-nothingness-becoming*. In the first moment, "being" is understood in terms of Platonic universals or abstract forms. Consciousness in the second moment comes to the realization that abstract universals without particulars are nonexistent, hence "nothingness." When, in the final moment, consciousness comes to see the whole picture as a process, the determination of becoming is finally understood as the concept and rationality of both being and nothingness. The Christian doctrine of God as the Trinity, for Hegel, is a representation of this truly philosophical concept of absolute spirit as a trinity of being, nothingness, and becoming. Hegel's treatment of Christianity is the topic to which we now turn.[54]

Hegel's Philosophy of Religion

The two previous sections have dealt with some overarching methodological themes in Hegel's philosophical system. With

54. The following section is expanded from a section in my "Church," in *The Oxford Handbook of Nineteenth-Century Christian Thought*, ed. J. Rasmussen, J. Wolfe, and J. Zachhuber (Oxford: Oxford University Press, 2017), 610–27.

regard to how he applies the method to the content, there are far too many areas to cover, but for the purposes of this book, I have chosen to focus on the philosophy of religion. "Religion" is the title of the penultimate chapter of the *Phenomenology of Spirit*, superseded, as it were, only by the final chapter titled "Absolute Knowledge." For many interpreters, this arrangement reflects the importance of religion to Hegel's system. Religion is arguably for Hegel the sphere of society and the moment of human consciousness closest to philosophy. Hegel calls Christianity "the true religion," "the absolute religion," and "the consummate religion," because he sees the contents of the Christian religion as identical to the philosophical truth of absolute idealism, albeit in representational form. It is important to note, however, that he has made some subtle but significant revisions to his philosophy of religion throughout the course of his career, so when we refer to "Hegel's philosophy of religion," we have to be specific about which version we are talking about. In what follows, I will focus on the latest discourse on the philosophy of religion that Hegel penned. The reader should bear in mind that this version of his philosophy of religion is not necessarily his most influential, but it is the most mature view that he developed during his career. The importance and indispensability that Hegel attached to Christianity at this stage of his philosophy of religion is, despite its fundamental disagreement with the central tenets of Christian theology, a powerful statement against the rapid secularization of Western Europe that he found profoundly worrisome.

From the *Phenomenology* to the 1827 Lectures

The issue at hand is whether established, institutional religions will ultimately be replaced by philosophy. According to the earlier Hegel, philosophy is the purpose of religion, and once that purpose has been fulfilled, religion will be sublated by philosophy. This understanding of religion has been appropriated by the Left Hegelians and later by Marxists, and is the view with which Hegel is more popularly associated. We will see, however, that the later Hegel in fact ascribes to religion a permanent status in the world.

Let us begin by recalling Hegel's distinction between representation and concept. Representational thinking is a form of understanding associated with sensibility, while conceptual thinking is to truly grasp the rational essence of something. In Hegel's idealist system, spirit is to be found in thought, not in sensibility, and since religion represents spirit through externally sensible elements, the task of lifting human consciousness to its conceptual form lies with philosophy and not religion.

Hegel's philosophy of religion can be outlined roughly as follows. He calls Christianity the "consummate religion" because its representations express the content of his philosophical system. In particular, the Christian doctrine of the incarnation gave rise to a consciousness of divine-human unity. This unity, sensibly represented by Christ as a particular human being, leads to the self-awareness of human consciousness as spirit and to the awareness that the divine-human nature of Christ belongs to the entire human race. This consciousness is not one that has only an absolute object in view, namely God. Rather, this consciousness as the subject is itself absolute in essence, because it is spirit's self-consciousness present in the consciousness of the spiritual community of the consummate religion.

That the Christian religion is only a representation of the truth of the absolute, however, does not mean for Hegel that Christianity is to be sublated through the dialectical transition into philosophy. True enough, the *Phenomenology of Spirit* (1807) presents religion as intrinsically alienating human beings from spirit because of its necessarily representational form. This alienation, as the early Hegel indicates, is overcome only by the transition from representation to concept. Even in the original

(1821) manuscript of his *Lectures on the Philosophy of Religion*, the ultimate subsection of the final part, titled "The Passing Away of the Community," indicates that the rationality of the consummate religion will be preserved, though the ecclesiastical priesthood will be replaced by the philosophical priesthood.[55]

In the 1824 manuscript of the same lectures, however, Hegel discards the aforementioned final section and replaces it with new material under the rubric of "The Realization of Faith." By 1827, he no longer ascribes any negative role to religion as that which philosophy sublates. To be sure, he still insists that religion is representational in form, but he no longer describes it as alienating. Rather, as early as 1824, he explicitly states that philosophy, in which the "sensibility" of religion is "developed and expanded," transforms the ecclesiastical community, rather than replacing it.[56]

Hegel's positive view of the consummate religion and the corresponding community is spelled out in detail in the 1827 manuscript of the religion lectures. This shift in his thinking is closely related to his increasing attention to the Christian community or *cultus*. In the 1821 manuscript, he sees the church, with her teachings of truth "from representation and from objectivity" that "awaken feelings," as a pedagogical community that *cultivates* (recall the Hegelian term *Bildung*) a representational consciousness of the absolute among the common folk.[57] In the *Phenomenology*, the central significance of dialectical-philosophical reconciliation as represented in Christianity lies with Christ, and when philosophy has uncovered the concept

---

55. See Georg Wilhelm Friedrich Hegel, *Lectures on the Philosophy of Religion*, vol. 3, *The Consummate Religion*, ed. Peter C. Hodgson (Oxford: Clarendon Press, 2007), 158. Hegel delivered these lectures in 1821, 1824, 1827, and 1831, with significant revisions each time.
56. Ibid., 237.
57. Ibid., 151.

of the divine-human unity expressed in the divine *and* human nature (singular!) of Christ, Christianity with its representational form seems to be no longer needed. With the shift of focus in his discussions of reconciliation from Christ to the community, however, the Hegel of 1824–27 is emphatically clear that the ecclesiastical aspect of the pedagogical community will not simply fade away, and that the church's continuing existence is justified by the philosophical priesthood.

The Consummate Religion

To see how Hegel arrives at this view of Christianity, we now turn to his 1827 lectures on the philosophy of religion as "the consummate religion." Characteristically, he divides his discussion (after an introduction) into three sections, each addressing one element, or moment, of that religion.

The first section is on "The Idea of God in and for Itself." Hegel writes: "In accord with the first element, then, we consider God in his eternal idea, as he is in and for himself, prior to or apart from the creation of the world, so to speak."[58] After briefly revisiting his famous reinterpretation of the Trinitarian doctrine, Hegel offers a highly innovative rendition of the Augustinian notion of God as love. For Augustine, love entails otherness; thus, the predication "God is love" implies three persons in the Godhead. Hegel applies this doctrine of God to his philosophical system of the divine-human unity: "This is love, and without knowing that love is both a distinguishing and the *sublation of the distinction*, one speaks emptily of it. This is the simple, eternal idea."[59]

The eternal idea of the triune God who is love, in whose life is self-differentiation, however, cannot be directly known to fallen human consciousness (hence the "so to speak") without

---

58. Ibid., 275.
59. Ibid., 276. Emphasis added.

reconciliation, and so it must first enter into historical human consciousness through "representation" and "appearance," which constitutes the "second element" of the consummate religion.[60] In this section, Hegel discusses the Christian narrative of the fall as representing the divine-human cleavage in spirit, and the narrative of reconciliation as the sublation of this cleavage, the establishment of the human consciousness of divine-human unity as spirit's self-consciousness.

Reconciliation as such is only partially accomplished in Christ, and its universal actualization pertains to the Christian community founded by the Holy Spirit, which Hegel discusses in the third section under the rubric of "The Third Element: Community, Spirit."[61] Reconciled consciousness, which is the consciousness of the absolute, is not only that of an absolute *object*, namely God. Rather, this consciousness as *subject* is itself essentially absolute, because it is spirit's self-consciousness present in the consciousness of the spiritual community.

The first subsection discusses the origin of this community, represented in the story of Pentecost as the outpouring of the Holy Spirit, which Hegel conceptualizes as "spirit that comprehends this history spiritually as it is enacted in appearance, and recognizes the idea of God in it, his life, his movement."[62] The resurrection, philosophically conceptualized as resurgence of the consciousness of divine-human unity in the spiritual community, is crucial for the initiation of the church.[63] This community is comprised of every empirical subject who is in spirit, but at the same time the history and truth of the community is objectified from its individual members upon the initiation of the church. The history of reconciliation "is something that is objective for

60. Ibid., 290–309.
61. Ibid., 328–29.
62. Ibid.
63. Ibid., 330.

them, and they must now traverse this history, this process, in themselves."[64] Only "by virtue of the fact that the subject traverses this process in itself" does it become "Spirit, and thus a citizen of the kingdom of God."[65]

In the second subsection, "The Subsistence of the Community," Hegel sets forth the view that "the Church is essentially a teaching Church."[66] He discusses a number of external ecclesiastical practices. Among all these representations, he gives primacy to doctrine: "Initially, doctrine is related to [the] individual as something external."[67] Yet, through ecclesial education (*Bildung*), the individual internalizes the truth that church dogmas represent. Once the members of the church appropriate the truth of the divine-human unity, they really partake "of the presence of God" in the Communion (the Lord's Supper), which completes the subsistence of the community.[68]

Meanwhile, there must also be a "transformation of the community" as a whole, which Hegel discusses in the final subsection of his 1827 lectures, titled "The Realization of the Spirituality of the Community."[69] The total, universal realization of the spirituality of the community requires the actualization of the same spirituality in the worldly realm, such that "the principle, the truth, of the worldly *is* the spiritual."[70]

After surveying the historical development of the community's spirituality in the world in the "real" and "ideal" dimensions, Hegel concludes that genuine reconciliation is actualized only when "the principle of freedom has penetrated into the worldly realm itself... because it has been... conformed to the concept,

64. Ibid., 329.
65. Ibid.
66. Ibid., 334.
67. Ibid., 335.
68. Ibid., 338.
69. Ibid., 339.
70. Ibid.

reason, and eternal truth,"[71] and when "subjectivity develops the content from itself" while knowing and recognizing "that a content is necessary and that this necessary content is objective."[72]

For Hegel, this final stage of reconciliation, which is "the standpoint of philosophy," does not sublate Christianity.[73] Rather, philosophy and philosophy alone is "capable of bearing witness to, and thus expressing the witness of, Spirit in a developed, thoughtful fashion. Therefore it is the justification of religion, especially of the Christian religion, the true religion."[74] Recognizing that philosophers will always be a minority, the later Hegel contends that Christianity in its consummate form as a "people's religion" (*Volksreligion*) will continue to be necessary in this world to teach the truth of reconciliation in representational form accessible to the common folk.

Conclusion

One observation we can gather from the foregoing discussions of Hegel's thought, against the background of the history of Western philosophy, is that the complexity and novelty of his system is hardly paralleled by any of his contemporaries or predecessors, with the possible exception of Kant. What this inevitably means is that the manifold implications of the method and content of Hegel's philosophy can be developed in many different directions. This is clearly evinced by the particular case of his philosophy of religion as developed in the immediately ensuing generation (thinkers born in the 1800s and 1810s). So-called Left Hegelians, or Young Hegelians, like Ludwig Feuerbach (1804–72), developed Hegel's view of religion in a

71. Ibid., 342.
72. Ibid., 345.
73. Ibid.
74. Ibid.

materialistic and atheistic direction, seeing religion as a necessary moment in history eventually to be sublated. On the other hand, theologians like Hans Lassen Martensen (1808–84), a Danish bishop best known today for having been a major adversary of his countryman Søren Kierkegaard (1813–55), found strong support in Hegel's system for established Christianity. Those familiar with the history of Dutch Calvinism may have come across the name of Johannes Scholten (1811–85), a Leiden theologian who had a significant influence on his student Herman Bavinck (1854–1921). Scholten, too, tried to integrate Hegel's idealism with the Reformed faith. Bavinck himself drew some insight from Scholten's version of Hegelianism, but was also severely critical of it.

In view of these widely varying developments of the complex implications of Hegel's thought, we may conclude this section by saying that any adequate and helpful assessment of his philosophy as a whole should consciously steer away from any simplistic "friend or foe" mind-set. His replacement of the triune God of Scripture with a logical trinity and his identification of the Christ figure as a representation of ultimate divine-human identity are obviously unacceptable to historically orthodox Christian traditions in general and the confessional Reformed faith in particular. Yet as we proceed to offer a Reformed assessment of Hegel's thought, we must bear in mind the complexity of his system and be careful not to reduce it to these heterodox propositions. Without further ado, then, let us continue on to the next chapter of this book and examine Hegel's worldview in light of the Reformed worldview.

3

A REFORMED ASSESSMENT OF HEGEL'S THOUGHT

What Reformed Thinkers Have Learned from Hegel

One thing on which great modern Reformed thinkers like Herman Bavinck and Cornelius Van Til would agree with Hegel is the understanding that no human thought can escape the truth of God, and that no system of philosophy can be without any element of truth. Of course, Calvin had already taught this. The Genevan Reformer tells us that there is an "awareness of divinity" (*sensus divinitatis*) within every human mind, "and indeed by natural instinct."[1] However corrupt, the "seed of religion" can "in no wise be uprooted."[2] What Hegel has given to modern Reformed thinkers is, as we shall see, a modern way of thinking and speaking, with which to articulate this historic doctrine of general revelation. In the meantime, they are constantly reminded by Calvin's caveat that non-Christians "may chance to

---

1. John Calvin, *Institutes of the Christian Religion*, ed. John T. McNeill, trans. Ford Lewis Battles, 2 vols. (Philadelphia: Westminster Press, 1960), 1.3.1, 1:43.
2. Ibid., 1.3.1, 1:51.

sprinkle their books with droplets of truth . . . [but] they saw things in such a way that their seeing did not direct them to the truth, much less enable them to attain it."[3]

One implication of these basic principles of the Reformed theological tradition is that a good theologian would never assess the thought of Hegel or any other thinker with a simplistic "friend or foe" mind-set. A better model of assessment would be to liken Hegel's thought to a shipwreck—that of one of the grandest ships ever built. Great Reformed theologians like Bavinck and Van Til would see their task as looking for all the treasures they can possibly salvage, so that these treasures may be brought back to where they properly belong.

It does not take the genius of a Herman Bavinck or a Charles Hodge to figure out that the god of Hegel's philosophy—"spirit," "the divine," "the absolute," or whatever—is a philosophical notion that differs fundamentally from the true God who revealed himself in nature and Scripture. The first question we need to ask before proceeding, then, is: does this mean that Hegel's philosophical speech about God is entirely irrelevant to the Christian's faithful proclamation of the God of Scripture?

Calvin's theology of revelation would remind us here that Christians and non-Christians alike are born with the aforementioned "sense of divinity," such that no rational creature can escape the idea of God. In one sense, the god of Hegelian philosophy is not the true, living God. In another sense, however, Hegel and Calvin are in fact seeking understanding of the same God innately revealed to the human mind, even though the former does so with unaided fallen reason, and the latter does so in the light of Scripture by faith. Without the inward illumination of the Holy Spirit and the light of God's Word, one can never make sense of one's inborn awareness of God. Yet the very awareness

3. Ibid., 2.2.18, 1:277.

of God that even the non-Christian seeks to explicate on false presuppositions is nonetheless still a notion of the true God. Put another way, nonbelievers hold to false notions of the true God, and in this limited sense, when they speak of God, they speak not of some false god or gods, but of the true God, albeit falsely. No creature can escape the truth of God. Because the natural, instinctual sense of divinity is revealed to the minds of all God's rational creatures (Rom. 1:18–21), it provides a point of contact, so to speak, on which Christians can engage non-Christians in dialogues about God.

In bringing the Christian worldview into contact with non-Christian worldviews, it is theologically imperative that, on the basis of general revelation, we find the right materials and terminologies to aid our conversation. This is because dogmatics, as the science of the church, belongs in the church; its contents need to be communicated in different ways in other fields of knowledge and spheres of society in accordance with their respective created orders. As we shall see, the great modern Reformed theologians whom we are about to discuss have found that Hegel's ideas and terminological framework, like the pagan notion of the "unknown God" (Acts 17:23) and the philosophical poetry of Epimenides and Aratus (Acts 17:28), can serve as an effective vehicle for communicating the Christian worldview to secular societies in public settings on a wide variety of subjects.

When we talk about what theologians have "learned" from Hegel, then, what I have in mind first of all is a modern framework of thought and communication. Yet there is more than that. In the Old Testament, God often raises up pagans to remind his people of what he has already taught them. Similarly, throughout the history of the church, Christian theology has repeatedly departed from some fundamental truths of revelation. In the modern era of Western thought, for example, "the incomprehensibility of God had been almost totally forgotten by theology."[4] Bavinck points out that it was "philosophy" that "rose up to remind us of this truth."[5] Of course, Hegel reacted against this Kantian philosophy of divine incomprehensibility, but this was because this non-Christian rendition of divine incomprehensibility was tantamount to unknowability—"philosophical agnosticism," in Bavinck's words.[6] Hegel's non-Christian corrective to Kant's critical philosophy was not an answer that Reformed theology could accept, yet theologians like Kuyper, Bavinck, Vos, Ridderbos, and Van Til saw elements in it that would serve as reminders of important truths of revelation for Christian theologians. Let us now see some examples of what great Reformed theologians critically appropriated from Hegel.

Herman Bavinck and Organicism

There are many elements of Hegelian philosophy that the Dutch neo-Calvinist Herman Bavinck (1854–1921) incorporated into his own theological program. Because organicism is a topic we discussed in some detail in chapter 2, I have chosen this as an example of what Bavinck picked up from Hegel.[7] It has to be emphasized from the outset that Bavinck's organicism differs fundamentally from Hegel's. James Eglinton rightly sums up the philosopher's view: "Hegel's organicism leads to monism and understands the *telos* of organicism in that light. His organicism is also closely related to his overall panentheistic concerns."[8]

---

4. Herman Bavinck, *Reformed Dogmatics*, ed. John Bolt, trans. John Vriend, 4 vols. (Grand Rapids: Baker, 2003–8), 2:41.
5. Ibid.
6. Ibid., 2:41–47.
7. Bavinck's organicism is far more sophisticated than can be adequately introduced here. For further treatment of this topic, see James Eglinton, *Trinity and Organism: Towards a New Reading of Herman Bavinck's Organic Motif* (London: T&T Clark, 2012).
8. Eglinton, *Trinity and Organism*, 66.

Bavinck's organicism, by contrast, interprets the universe as an organic whole, using the central motif of unity-in-diversity modeled after the triune God, which presupposes a strict Creator-creature distinction in which God is the archetype and creation the ectype. In this way Bavinck clearly distinguishes himself from Hegel's absolute idealism.

Yet there are important things on which Bavinck would, in one way or another, agree with Hegel as well. In chapter 2, we discussed how Hegel's organicism constitutes a refutation of substance metaphysics. According to substance metaphysics, a thing is what it is by virtue of its static form or nature. A thing actually becomes what it could potentially be by a mechanical order of causes and effects. The mechanical laws of causation are what govern the operations of the universe. Against the mechanical view of the universe propounded by substance metaphysics, Hegel proposes to see the universe as a living organism, a subject living the process of its life.

Bavinck also recognizes the problematic "tendency towards substance"—as Hegel would put it—of traditional metaphysics, which finds its basis in the mechanical laws of natural causality. Bavinck points out that this mechanical worldview is ultimately materialistic and atheistic. Atheistic "materialism" envisions the universe as "a mechanism that is brought about by the union and separation of atoms."[9] He is troubled by the way theology is often done upon mechanistic presuppositions.[10]

Like Hegel, however, Bavinck does not simply jettison substantialist thought altogether. Just as Hegel recognizes the fixity of universals as a moment integral to the truth as a whole, Bavinck retains the traditional understanding of natures as the formal-causal attributes that distinguish one kind of creatures

---

9. Bavinck, *Reformed Dogmatics*, 2:435.
10. Ibid., 612.

from another: "Everything was created with a *nature of its own* and rests in ordinances established by God."[11] Yet Bavinck, with Hegel, sees the need to reinterpret the traditional notion of substances as *living* substances, rather than as mechanical parts of an inorganic universe.

To that end, Bavinck insists that the laws of causality must be understood anew in organicist light. He does not simply reject or abandon the notion of causality in traditional metaphysics, but insists that this notion makes sense only if it is understood within a truly theistic, rather than naturalistic, framework. It is "the confession of God as the Creator of heaven and earth that immediately brings with it the one absolute and never self-contradictory truth, the harmony and beauty of the counsel of God, and hence the unity of the cosmic plan and the order of all of nature."[12] Citing the German philosopher and sociologist Friedrich Albert Lange's (1823–75) work on materialism, Bavinck insists that only on the basis of the "full scope of nature" as such, in which "one attributes to the one God also a unified manner of working," can "the connectedness of things in terms of cause and effect" become not only "conceivable but even a necessary consequence of the assumption."[13] This, says Bavinck, is the "natural order" that "Scripture itself models to us" concerning "a wide range of ordinances and laws for created things."[14]

In so rejecting the mechanical view of the universe with Hegel, however, Bavinck refuses to adopt the idealist alternative. Bavinck describes the Hegelian worldview as "pantheistic" (this is not entirely accurate—"panentheistic" would be closer to the truth—but let us just take it as it is). He observes that "pantheism attempts to explain the world dynamically; materialism

11. Ibid., 435. Emphasis added.
12. Ibid., 612.
13. Ibid.
14. Ibid.

attempts to do so mechanically. But both strive to see the whole as governed by a single principle."[15] This is precisely what he finds problematic in both Hegel's system and the worldview that the philosopher rejects: both fail to recognize God as the Creator of the universe and are thus ultimately atheistic. Bavinck explains:

> In pantheism the world may be a living organism . . . of which God is the soul; in materialism it is a mechanism that is brought about by the union and separation of atoms. But in both systems an unconscious blind fate is elevated to the throne of the universe. Both fail to appreciate the richness and diversity of the world. . . . Both deny the existence of a conscious purpose and cannot point to a cause or a destiny for the existence of the world and its history.[16]

In a "deadly bath of uniformity," both of these worldviews "erase the boundaries" between different natures within creation—"heaven and earth, matter and spirit, soul and body, man and animal," etc.—as well as the qualitative distinction between "Creator and creature."[17] The treasure of organicism salvaged from Hegel's shipwreck, as it were, insists Bavinck, must be brought into the light of "Scripture's worldview that is radically different."[18]

According to the biblical worldview, God created everything according to its own nature and continues to sustain the distinctions between different kinds of things. "Sun, moon, and stars have their own unique task; plants, animals, and humans are distinct in nature. There is the most profuse diversity and yet, in that diversity, there is also a superlative kind of unity."[19]

15. Ibid., 435.
16. Ibid.
17. Ibid.
18. Ibid.
19. Ibid., 435–36.

This unity-diversity dialectic is modeled after the triune God. However, the universe is not an emanation of God's being—nor is it God's being itself, developing in a trinitarian mode of logical moments through history. Bavinck maintains the strictest distinction between God and creatures: "The foundation of both diversity and unity is in God. It is he who created all things . . . , who continually upholds them in their distinctive natures."[20]

Here, then, "is a unity that does not destroy but rather maintains diversity, and a diversity that does not come at the expense of unity, but rather unfolds it in its riches."[21] The manifest unity and diversity of the universe for which Hegel attempted to account is something that "neither the mechanical principle of materialism nor" Hegel's own "dynamic principle . . . is sufficient to explain."[22] In Hegel's idealism, "God has no existence and life of his own apart from the world. . . . In the thought of Hegel . . . , the Absolute, pure Being, Thought, Idea, does not exist before the creation of the world, but is only logically and potentially prior to the world."[23] Despite Hegel's avowed commitment to focus on the concrete developments of history, therefore, "all the qualifications of the Absolute" are ultimately "devoid of content—nothing but abstract logical categories."[24] That is, the concrete existence of every individual subject and every kind of things is ultimately reduced to a logical trinity that has no existence of its own apart from particular creatures, rather than the self-existent Trinity.

Bavinck insists that only in light of the living, triune God, with his lively work of creation, can we make sense of the organic unity and diversity of this universe that is clearly manifested to us. It is on this basis that he develops a distinctively Christian

20. Ibid., 436.
21. Ibid.
22. Ibid.
23. Ibid., 177.
24. Ibid.

version of organicism: "In virtue of this unity," which finds its foundation in the one triune God, "the world can, metaphorically, be called an organism, in which all the parts are connected with each other and influence each other reciprocally."[25] Bavinck interprets these organic relations with the Chalcedonian pattern of inseparable unity and abiding distinction: "Heaven and earth, man and animal, soul and body, truth and life, art and science, religion and morality, state and church, family and society, and so on, though they are all distinct, are not separated."[26] This understanding of unity and diversity neatly sums up the organicism that Bavinck salvaged from Hegel and incorporated into a Reformed rendition of the Christian worldview: "There is a wide range of connections between them; an organic . . . bond holds them all together."[27] In what follows, we shall see how Geerhardus Vos and Cornelius Van Til further developed these insights that Bavinck critically appropriated from Hegel.

Geerhardus Vos on the Organic Nature of Biblical Revelation

As mentioned in chapter 2, Geerhardus Vos (1862–1949) was another strong proponent of theological organicism. As a dogmatician, he is often honored as the father of Reformed biblical theology. While Vos seldom cites or engages with Hegel explicitly, those familiar with the writings of Hegel and subsequent German idealists would recognize Vos's extensive use of their organicist language. The fact that he quietly "strained to differentiate his own use of the organic from that of German idealism" may be taken as a hint that he consciously and critically appropriated elements of Hegelian organicism and incorporated them into both his dogmatic view of biblical revelation and his exegesis of the

25. Ibid., 436.
26. Ibid.
27. Ibid.

Bible.[28] Though Vos does not explicitly state his purpose in borrowing the language and thought-form of Hegelian organicism, the way he uses them, as we shall see, is clearly polemical against the kind of philosophy that rejects or shuns God's self-revelation in Scripture as well as in nature and history.

Whereas Hegel sees the history of the universe as inherently *divine* because of its ultimate identity with the god of his philosophy, Vos insists that the same history is inherently *revelatory*, but is in no sense identical with the divine being or endowed with even a trace of God's own nature. Rather, the history of the creaturely universe is God's work external (*ad extra*) to his being. The biblical account of redemptive history as the creation-fall-redemption triad is the only light through which the history of the world can be truly understood. The key point regarding Vos's critical appropriation of Hegelian organicism, then, is his un-Hegelian and even anti-Hegelian insistence upon the necessity of revelation as God's act *ad extra*, never to be confused with God's being *ad intra*, for true and adequate knowledge of God and of the history of the universe that he created.

Historic Reformed theology places a strong emphasis on the *propositional* nature of biblical revelation (i.e., "propositional revelation"): when God inspired the authors of the Bible to reveal himself, he spoke the living truth of his being and works in propositional form. Consider these familiar examples: "I am who I am" (Ex. 3:14); "God is spirit" (John 4:24); "God is light" (1 John 1:5); "God is love" (1 John 4:8; 4:16); "God created the heavens and the earth" (Gen. 1:1). The propositional nature of biblical revelation allows us to explicate its truths systematically on distinct topics, such as God, creation, the atonement, and the application of salvation.

---

28. Eglinton, *Trinity and Organism*, 61. See also Brian Mattson, *Restored to Our Destiny: Eschatology and the Image of God in Herman Bavinck's* Reformed Dogmatics (Leiden: Brill, 2012), 46n151–52.

Vos uses Hegel's organicist thought-form to argue that the truthful propositions revealed in Scripture are organic parts of the living truth. It has to be emphasized at once that Vos does not subscribe to Hegel's monistic organicism, which treats God (the absolute) and revelation (history) as identical. Vos's biblical theology presupposes a standard Reformed understanding of the Creator-creature distinction, such that the redemptive history of the creaturely world is not the unfolding of God's *being*, but rather an *act of revelation* of God's nature through his works that are external to his being. Despite this fundamental disagreement, however, the organicism of Hegel and German idealism has provided Vos with a powerful way to express his caveat against the dangers of dissecting God's truth into dismembered parts and treating them as mechanical and inorganic components.

In one passage, Vos appeals to Jesus as the supreme model of a biblical exegete. He notes that Jesus fully exploits the propositional character of the Old Testament such that "he does not essentially differ from those whose treatment of prophecy is often stigmatized as literalistic and mechanical."[29] In defending the propositional model of biblical interpretation, however, Vos stresses that "the Old Testament was to Him [Jesus] an *organic expression* of the truth and will of God."[30] Elsewhere he describes the believer's union with Christ, a dogmatic truth central to the doctrine of salvation, as an "organic mystical union."[31] Because the propositional truths revealed in Scripture constitute the *living* truth of God manifested through the process of redemptive history, dogmatic theology must, in Vos's view, also reflect this organic nature.

Vos's biblical theology focuses on the creation-fall-redemption

---

29. Geerhardus Vos, *Biblical Theology: Old and New Testaments* (Eugene, OR: Wipf and Stock, 2003), 359.
30. Ibid. Emphasis added.
31. Ibid., 385.

triad of the *process* of redemptive *history*. The italicized terms here reflect elements strongly reminiscent of Hegel. In fact, Vos's discussion of "the organic nature of the historic process observable in revelation" is fraught with Hegelian terminology, which he employs without adopting any substantive aspect of Hegelian ontology.[32]

He may agree in some sense with Hegel's post-Kantian presupposition that our consciousness does not possess the capacity to know anything except through observable nature and history. Historic Reformed theology, on the basis of the theological axiom that *finitum non capax infiniti* (the finite is incapable of knowing the infinite), teaches that even in Eden, Adam could not have known God immediately. Adam knew God only through his mediatory self-revelation through his handiworks, including God's speech to Adam in *human* language. Human knowledge of God "became possible" only through his revelatory work of creation.[33]

Vos would even agree in some sense with the Kantian view that human beings cannot attain any knowledge of God through the study of nature by unaided reason. However, in Vos's creation-fall-redemption framework, this human incapacity is a result of the fall. Historic Reformed theology teaches that fallen human beings cannot understand God's revelation (*homo peccator non capax verbi divini*). Nature and history are revelatory, and this only renders human beings inexcusable for not knowing God. Yet, because human reason is fallen, human beings cannot know God without his verbal revelation to us in creaturely language about his supranatural and supratemporal being. Thus, Vos stresses that "the indispensableness of revelation stands or falls with the recognition of the fact of sin."[34]

For no good reason, the category of revelation is entirely

32. Ibid., 7.
33. Ibid., 4.
34. Ibid.

foreign to Hegel's system (and also Kant's, for that matter). Hegel, with his post-Kantian presuppositions, holds that a divine being transcendent to the world is unknowable to autonomous human reason. Hegel's strategy of establishing God's knowability, as we have seen, is to identify natural world history with the very life of God's being. This is a starting point that Vos firmly rejects.

Vos's solution is to identify divine revelation as an act of God that is external to, and yet deeply reflective of, his being. This analogical correspondence between God's works *ad extra* and his being *ad intra* finds its center in Jesus Christ, who is fully and truly God and human in one unabridged person—hence, the "Christocentric" character of Reformed biblical theology after Vos.[35]

Vos emphasizes that history is revelational, and revelation is historical (as does Bavinck[36]). This allows him to differentiate himself from Hegel, who thinks that history is divine and the divine is historical. What Vos has learned from Hegel is that the ahistorical and atemporal became knowable to human beings only by becoming historical and temporal. History as such is inherently supernatural and miraculous (so says Bavinck as well), but, contra Hegel, not divine.

The distinctively Reformed rendition of Chalcedonian Christology allows Vos to draw the connection between the ahistorical-atemporal being of God and his temporal-historical self-revelation without falling into Hegel's monistic philosophy of divine-human identity. Reformed Christology characteristically emphasizes the distinction between Christ's two natures more than any other major theological tradition, and this is a result of the Reformed insistence upon the Creator-creature distinction. For instance, when Lutheran theologians in the period

---

35. See ibid., 343–46.
36. See, for example, Bavinck, *Reformed Dogmatics*, 2:339–42.

of high orthodoxy insisted that the human flesh and blood of Christ could be at the right hand of the Father and on the communion table at the same time by means of some sacramental union, Reformed theologians countered this view by insisting that Christ, according to his human nature, has never been and will never become omnipresent as God. Scholastic Lutheran theologians ridiculed this consistent emphasis on the abiding distinction between Christ's two natures with the epithet *extra Calvinisticum*. Part and parcel of this *extra* is the Reformed rejection of the Lutheran understanding of the "majestic genus" (*genus maiestaticum*) as a category of the communication of attributes (*communicatio idiomatum*). Lutheran orthodoxy would, for example, think that the Christ-child in the manger already knew the Torah because the omniscience of his divine nature was communicated to his human nature. Reformed Christology rejects this view and insists that Christ, according to his humanity, was never and will never become omniscient as God. While Vos does not go into these dogmatic details in his *Biblical Theology*, the characteristically Reformed shape of his Christology is clear in the third volume of his *Reformed Dogmatics*.[37] This Reformed distinction between Christ's two natures on the basis of the Creator-creature distinction gives Vos an immunity against Hegelian infections when he draws upon Hegel's insights.

Vos starts off the section under the rubric of "the organic nature of the historic process observable in revelation" by stating that "every increase is *progressive*, but not every progressive increase bears an organic character."[38] He then goes on to explicate the doctrine of *progressive revelation* as an *organic* process. This Reformed doctrine teaches us that God's special revelation was not given to his people all at once, but rather progressively

---

37. Geerhardus Vos, *Reformed Dogmatics*, vol. 3, *Christology* (Bellingham: Lexham Press, 2015). See especially chapter 3 of the volume.

38. Vos, *Biblical Theology*, 7.

through the history of redemption. This view of revelation can be open to the substantialist charge that it "excludes its absolute perfection at all stages."[39] The classical, substantialist mind would think of the truth of the universe as a static whole, completely available to human reason at all points of history.

The immanent, eternal truth of God-in-himself is of course always perfectly and purely actual and totally immutable. But because this truth, mediated to subjective human knowledge through the history of God's works, is his very *living* truth, its revelation takes on the character of *progression* (Vos follows Bavinck's critical recalibration of the idealist term "mediation"—which of course originated in biblical terminology—to describe revelation[40]). Revelation of the truth is organic, because the truth revealed is the living truth of God and his works. Only "if the progress" of revelation "were non-organic" would the "absolute perfection" of revelation "at all stages" be compromised.[41]

Vos, like Hegel, explains the notion of "organic progress" with the analogy of plant growth. This progress "is from seed-form to the attainment of full growth; yet we do not say that in the qualitative sense the seed is less perfect than the tree."[42] Critically adopting Hegel's dialectical division of history into different stages, Vos claims that the extent of special revelation given at each stage of redemptive history fulfills the criterion of "soteric sufficiency of the truth."[43]

In the "first state" of the "emergence" of special revelation, the limited extent of the truth revealed was already sufficient for our ancestors to attain salvation.[44] This is because "in the seed-form

---

39. Ibid.
40. For example, Vos, *Biblical Theology*, 343; Bavinck, *Reformed Dogmatics*, 2:310. Bavinck stresses that "all revelation is mediate."
41. Vos, *Biblical Theology*, 7.
42. Ibid.
43. Ibid.
44. Ibid.

the minimum of indispensable knowledge was already present."[45] In other words, the whole truth of revelation was already contained in the seed in an implicit form.

What Vos means is that revealed truths were not given as dismembered chunks or mechanical parts during the successive stages of history, as if God gave to Abraham, Isaac, and Jacob the wheels of a car; to Moses, the frame; to the prophets, the windows; in and through Jesus, the engine; and finally to the apostles, the rest of the parts. The organic nature of revelation means that the truth is given as a whole from the very beginning: the seed is the whole of the plant in implicit form. The accumulation of later revelations was not the *addition* of mechanical parts, but the *growth* of one single, organic unity.

As special revelation progresses organically in the history of redemption, it manifests an "increasing multiformity" characteristic of "the development of organic life."[46] Here again Vos sounds a lot like Hegel. Recall that Hegel insists that truth is both absolute and multiform, and that seeming contradictions in the progression of the truth are merely apparent.

Vos, however, rejects Hegel's understanding of the progression of the truth itself. For Vos, the truth of God does not progress. The truth of God is eternal and immutable. *Revelation of the truth is progressive in its historical character; the truth of God's being* is not. Revelation consists of the *works* of God *ad extra*, which perfectly manifest, but are not identical to, God's being. Vos, like Bavinck, places a strong accent on the distinction between the truth of God's inner being and the outward revelation of this truth, a distinction integral to the Creator-creature distinction. Revelation, as an act of God external to his being, takes place within the creaturely world.

45. Ibid.
46. Ibid.

Critically adopting the language and thought-form of Hegelian organicism, Vos explains that the "variableness and differentiation in the Bible" are fully compatible with "its absoluteness and infallibility."[47] The ostensible contradictions are not real contradictions. They are merely the manifestation of the multiformity of revelation, which follows from the richness and complexity of the truth revealed.[48] This richness and complexity exist in harmonious simplicity in God himself (to borrow Hegel's language—*an sich*), but when it is *differentiated* (to utilize Hegel's terminology again) from God and communicated to creatures in the form of history, it becomes ostensibly *dialectical* in its manifestation.

Note that Vos does not use the Hegelian term "dialectical" to describe historical revelation.[49] Rather, he uses this term in association with *deism* (the view that the Creator does not intervene in his creation, so that all events in creation must be understood naturalistically).[50] On the "Deistical" view, the seemingly paradoxical character of historical revelation as reflected in Paul's "dialectic mentality" constitutes a "hindrance for the ideal communication of the message."[51]

Vos presupposes, over against deism, a theistic worldview—that Christianity is the only truly theistic worldview. On this view, "the truth" has "inherently many sides, and God" has "access to and control of all intended *organs* of revelation."[52] Contra Hegel, Vos insists that God is not identical with revelation; the latter is

47. Ibid., 8.
48. Ibid.
49. Ibid.
50. This association between deism and what Hegel would call the dialectical moment of logic seems to suggest that Vos had already discovered the critical Kantian presuppositions underlying Hegel's metaphysics. If that is true, Vos's understanding of Hegel would lie somewhere between the post-Kantian and the revised metaphysical schools of interpretation (see chapter 2).
51. Vos, *Biblical Theology*, 8.
52. Ibid. Emphasis added.

God's "production of extra-divine knowledge," and God's being *ad intra* and acts *ad extra* remain distinct.[53] God existed prior to revelation: "Originally God alone existed. He was known to Himself alone, and had first to call into being a creature before any *extraneous* knowledge with regard to Him became possible."[54] God is the Creator and master of the historical medium of revelation. This is what ensures the trustworthiness of revelation: God is in control of this historical medium, and he "shaped" each organ thereof "for the precise purpose to be served."[55]

The "precise, doctrinal structure" of biblical revelation, which provides the basis for systematic theology, is precisely the result of the organic nature of the redemptive history that the Bible reveals.[56] In our day and age, many biblical scholars—some of them Reformed—refer to systematic theology as "frozen dogmatics," and refuse to reflect upon biblical revelation with systematic, analytical mentalities. "Organic" and "systematic" are often seen as antonyms. For Vos, however, biblical theology's organic nature serves as the basis for clear, systematic expressions of the truth in dogmatic theology. This is precisely what he means by his famous statement that biblical theology is a "handmaid" to systematic theology.[57]

Cornelius Van Til and the Concrete Universal

In the two previous examples, we considered Reformed appropriations of Hegel's organicism. An important notion integral to Hegel's organicism is that of the "**concrete universal**," which Cornelius Van Til (1895–1987) critically incorporated

---

53. Ibid., 4.
54. Ibid.
55. Ibid., 8.
56. Ibid.
57. Geerhardus Vos, "The Idea of Biblical Theology as a Science and as a Theological Discipline," in *Redemptive History and Biblical Interpretation*, ed. Richard B. Gaffin, Jr. (Phillipsburg, NJ: Presbyterian and Reformed, 1980), 23–24.

into his presuppositionalist epistemology. In chapter 2, we discussed the terms "concrete" and "universal" in the philosopher's writings, but have not yet introduced the notion of the concrete universal.

In classical philosophy, "universals" are distinguished from "particulars." When I say, "This cat is small," it refers to a *particular* cat that happens to be small. By contrast, when I say, "Cats are adorable," I am speaking *universally* of a biological species. Although Plato and Aristotle prioritize the relations between universals and particulars differently, they are in agreement that universals are defined or, in Hegel's language, determined (*bestimmt*—see chapter 2) by, their *abstract* forms. This method of *abstraction*, as applied to the study of universals and particulars, as we have seen, underlies the *substantialist* ways of thinking that are characteristic of traditional metaphysics.

There are several problems with substantialist abstraction. In our discussion of Bavinck's organicism, we saw how this leads to a mechanistic view of the universe as consisting of lifeless substances operating in accordance with the abstract laws of causality. Here we may proceed with this observation and note how Hegel points out that substances or beings abstractly conceived in terms of universals are, as a matter of fact, nonexistent: the abstract form of, say, cats is not an actual existence like this or that particular cat.

It is worth explaining here that Reformed orthodoxy has traditionally followed Aristotle's view of particulars in relation to universals and rejected Plato's. Plato thinks that universal forms really exist, and are ontologically prior to particulars. Aristotle, by contrast, insists that universals do not exist apart from particulars. As we saw in chapter 2, Hegel deeply admired Aristotle and sought to develop many of the classical philosopher's latent ideas. It is thus unsurprising that Aristotelian influences on seventeenth-century Reformed scholasticism and on Hegel would converge in modern Dutch Calvinism on this specific point. Bavinck's understanding of particulars and universals is a typical example: "Abstractions—universals—do not exist in reality. The tree, the human being, the science, the language, the religion, the theology are nowhere to be found. Only particular trees, human beings, sciences, languages, and religions exist."[58]

In asserting the nonexistence of abstract universals, Van Til follows Bavinck in taking a historic Reformed starting point to adopt Hegel's agreement with Aristotle critically. Hegel's criticism of abstract thinking, however, does not stop here. Abstract thinking not only leads to nonexistent abstract universals, but also to "abstract particulars" that annihilate "being" in another way.

Let us consider the being of a cat again. To consistently and thoroughly honor the particularity of a cat, one would be forced to give up the abstract universal and speak of *this* cat and *that* cat in two different senses of the word "cat." But in this case the word "cat" loses its concrete definition/determination, and each individual cat becomes an abstract particular. That is to say, the noun "cat" is now emptied of its meaning, and so we can no longer meaningfully designate this or that particular cat as a "cat" in any concretely determined sense. When we say that this *is* a cat or what not, the "is" has now become abstract and meaningless.

This dilemma is what characterizes the second moment of logic of which Hegel speaks (see chapter 2). In this moment, the abstract determination of *being* from the previous moment is carried into *nothingness*. At a famous "juncture" where Van Til "introduce[s]" the Hegelian term "concrete universal," he adopts Hegel's very own criticism of *abstract* thinking in the framework of the unity-and-diversity, or "one-and-many," question:

58. Herman Bavinck, *Reformed Dogmatics*, 1:85.

The *many* must be brought into contact with one another. But . . . how do we know that the many do no simply exist as unrelated particulars? The answer given is that in such a case we should know nothing of them; they would be abstracted from the body of knowledge that we have; they would be *abstract* particulars. On the other hand, how is it possible that we should obtain a unity that does not destroy the particulars? We seem to get our unity by generalizing, by abstracting from the particulars in order to include them into larger unities. If we keep up this process of generalization till we exclude all particulars, granted they can all be excluded, have we then not stripped these particulars of their particularity? Have we then obtained anything but an *abstract* universal?[59]

Van Til acknowledges that "the notion of the concrete universal has been offered by idealist philosophy in order to escape the *reductio ad absurdum* of the abstract particular and the abstract universal."[60] Hegel's dialectical solution is a mediation between being and nothingness, namely, the third logical moment of *becoming*. In this final moment, the universal is no longer understood abstractly. Rather, it is construed as a concrete subject with itself as the object of its own consciousness, in itself and for itself. In other words, the universal is conceptually (rather than representationally) comprehended as absolute spirit (i.e., spirit in its fully actualized moment) as a concrete living substance.

This identification of absolute spirit as the concrete universal serves to underscore the view that the particular things and substances making up the whole of the universe are not static and mutually unrelated parts, but rather are integral to the life of spirit as a whole. It is the life of the concrete universal that gives

---

59. Cornelius Van Til, *The Defense of the Faith* (Phillipsburg, NJ: P&R Publishing, 2008), 48–49.
60. Ibid., 49.

purpose and meaning to each particular substance in each phase of the historical process of its development. The concrete universal is the organic unity of every particular thing, and it makes every particular meaningfully related to all others.

One implication of Hegel's notion of the concrete universal is this: whether or not we are consciously aware of it, whether we like it or not, each one of us inescapably participates in the whole truth of spirit. Only in light of the concrete universal can we make sense of our particular existences and experiences.

This is where Hegel and Van Til appear to sound alike. For Van Til, every human mind is endowed with an intrinsic awareness of God. Christians and non-Christians alike participate in the truth of God and his creation. Only in light of this truth can the human mind make sense of the reality that we perceive. Unregenerate reason that rejects the truth of God necessarily ends up in the kind of abstract contradictions that Hegel identified.

Van Til, like Hegel, holds that the one-and-many question can only be answered in light of the notion of a concrete universal. However, insists Van Til, "it is only in the Christian doctrine of the triune God, as we are bound to believe, that we really have a *concrete universal*. In God's being there are no particulars not related to the universal and there is nothing universal that is not fully expressed in the particulars."[61]

Van Til points out that in spite of Hegel's commitment to thinking concretely, the German philosopher's notion of the concrete universal is still a construct of abstract reasoning. In Hegel's system, particularity is annihilated by the universal that is the absolute. Van Til arrives at the same conclusion as Bavinck with exactly the same reasoning we saw earlier: in Hegel's idealism, all predications of the absolute are ultimately devoid of content.[62]

61. Ibid. Emphasis original.
62. Cornelius Van Til, *An Introduction to Systematic Theology*, ed. William Edgar (Phillipsburg, NJ: P&R Publishing, 2007), 292.

Only the Christian worldview is capable of thinking of God and thereby of the world concretely. For Van Til, concrete thinking is what sets the Christian worldview apart from non-Christian worldviews, which unavoidably think of God and the world in abstract terms. Van Til points out that, in Hegelian language, "if one thinks abstractly, one obtains a negative, empty essence."[63] This is precisely Hegel's criticism of traditional substance metaphysics: the moment of abstraction unavoidably evolves into the moment of the negatively rational in which being is annihilated. Van Til adds that "this essence is then contrasted to positive thought content that is said, in the nature of the case, to delimit the essence."[64] Here I take him to be alluding to Hegel's "speculative or positively rational moment of logic" that we discussed in chapter 2.

This logical moment is where Van Til's fundamental disagreement with Hegel emerges. The result of Hegel's positive rationality, says Van Til, is that the truly transcendent and self-existent God, if he exists, is still rendered rationally unknowable—the Kantian rendition of divine incomprehensibility as rational unknowability has not been overcome.[65] At the same time, human knowledge of the world and its history is equated to the knowledge of divinity. In other words, "a non-Christian notion of incomprehensibility is combined with a non-Christian notion of positive knowledge, and the result is a split in the Godhead as well as the destruction of human knowledge."[66]

Van Til does not explain in this passage how he arrives at the conclusion that abstract thinking ultimately leads to the destruction of human knowledge. This is a topic to which we shall return when we discuss his criticism of Hegel. For now, let us consider

63. Ibid., 323.
64. Ibid.
65. Ibid., 293–94.
66. Ibid., 323.

how Van Til salvages Hegel's notion of the concrete universal and incorporates it into a Christian worldview.

Van Til insists that only God can be called the concrete universal. Ontologically speaking (that is, speaking of God-in-himself), this statement applies both to God's triunity and to his attributes. Each person of the Godhead is a particular person, and yet each person possesses the fullness of God's being. Therefore, in the triune God every particular is fully the universal, and the universal is fully expressed in the particulars.

The case of the divine attributes named in Scripture reveals to us how God as the concrete universal is the light in which particulars in the creaturely world can be named, each according to its kind. Each divine attribute is particular and must be distinguished from others, but "we cannot divide up the Godhead."[67] Van Til is emphatic that "in dealing with distinctions in the Godhead, we must be careful not to do despite to the simplicity of his being."[68]

Yet we must not think of the distinctions of the attributes as mere inventions of our mind either. These are real distinctions in God's very being, which is indivisibly simple. Just as each person of the Godhead possesses the fullness of God's being, says Van Til, "each attribute of God is *coterminous* with God" (here he follows Bavinck very closely).[69] God is merciful, and he is righteous. God's mercy and righteousness are distinct attributes that are not to be confused. However, God's mercy is righteous, and his righteousness is merciful. Each of these attributes contains within it all the other attributes of God. The divine attributes are inseparable and yet without confusion, while the Godhead is without division and immutable. Each particular attribute is universal, and the universality of the Godhead is expressed in

67. Ibid.
68. Ibid.
69. Ibid. Emphasis added.

each of the particular attributes. In this way, God is self-existent as the concrete universal.

It has to be emphasized at once that God's self-existence means that he is, has always been, and always will be the concrete universal, with or without the creaturely world. A truly Christian worldview therefore

> begins with God as the concrete self-existent being. Thus God is not named according to what is found in the creature, except God has first named the creature according to what is in himself. The only reason why it appears as though God is named according to what is found in the creature is that, as creatures, we must psychologically begin with ourselves in our knowledge of anything. We are ourselves the proximate starting point of all our knowledge. In contrast to this, however, we should think of God as the ultimate starting point of knowledge. God is the archetype, while we are the ectype. God's knowledge is archetypal, and ours ectypal.[70]

This means that God, self-revealed through his works, is *the* concrete universal in light of which everything in this world makes sense. Van Til explains that "in every knowledge transaction, we must bring the particulars of our experience into relation with universals."[71] Yet unless we "presuppose God back of this world," our attempt to interpret the universe by "connecting the particulars and the universals" ultimately "leaves our knowledge at loose ends."[72]

The triune God is the "original one and many," and our creaturely universe is a "derivative one and many."[73] Without the

70. Ibid.
71. Ibid., 58.
72. Ibid., 59.
73. Ibid.

concretely revealed knowledge of God's triunity and of his relation to the world as its Creator, the problem of particulars and universals can only be tackled abstractly—this is so even in the case of Hegel, who rightly pointed out the dilemma of abstract thinking.

Van Til's presuppositionalism, then, can in this sense be seen as a Christian-theistic recalibration of Hegel's process-idealist treatment of universality and particularity. Van Til agrees with Hegel's criticism of classical Greek substantialism, but does not find Hegel's own solution viable. He critically appropriates Hegel's notion of the concrete universal and fleshes it out with truly Christian and truly theistic contents. When Van Til refers to God as the concrete universal, he has in mind the truth that only in light of the knowledge of the triune God given to us in biblical revelation can we noetically honor both the diversity and the unity of the world observable to us.

Francis Schaeffer and Cultural Apologetics

As a final and briefer example, we shall consider the more popular case of Francis Schaeffer's (1912–84) cultural apologetics. Schaeffer's writings might not be nearly as dogmatically and philosophically rigorous as those of Bavinck, Vos, and Van Til, but as far as popular influence is concerned, Schaeffer's apologetic method cannot be regarded as any less important than that of any other twentieth-century apologist. Among the luminaries of contemporary Reformed theology, Professor William Edgar of Westminster Theological Seminary is a foremost example of an apologist who has critically adopted Schaeffer's method. Another example in recent American evangelicalism is the late Charles Colson.

The formal, though certainly not substantive, aspect of Schaeffer's cultural apologetics is significantly informed by the idealist historicism handed down from Hegel. His celebrated

1976 book *How Should We Then Live?* resonates deeply with idealist concerns in two major questions that it seeks to answer: (1) how did our collective cultural consciousness get to where it is now, and (2) how does this historical process inform us about where we are going from here?[74]

Central to Schaeffer's cultural apologetics is his focus on the notion of the spirit of the age, or *Zeitgeist*. This is in fact characteristic of this genre of apologetics, which, "in its strictest sense . . . attempts to speak specifically to a *zeitgeist* [sic]."[75] Though Hegel did not coin the German compound word himself, he is rightly credited with having made this notion prominent in modern Western understandings of culture and history. Phrases like "spirit of the age(s)" and depictions of the spirit of specific periods of history occur throughout Hegel's works, most notably in *Lectures on the Philosophy of World History*.[76] In our exposition of Hegel's thought in chapter 2, we also saw how he repeatedly uses phrases like "the spirit of our time" in his writings.[77]

Unlike other mainstream European philosophers before him, Hegel does not approach metaphysical questions by discussing philosophical ideas *abstractly*. One key feature of Hegel's philosophy, as we have seen, is the way he traces the *concrete* expressions of these ideas in their sociopolitical and cultural settings in successive stages of history. In this way, he seeks to make sense of the world-spirit of specific eras by intellectually placing himself within the *Zeitgeist* of each historical stage.

Readers familiar with Schaeffer's writings can see here that

---

74. Francis Schaeffer, *How Should We Then Live? The Rise and Decline of Western Thought and Culture* (Wheaton, IL: Crossway, 2005).

75. "Cultural Apologetics," in *The Popular Encyclopedia of Apologetics*, ed. Ed Hindson and Ergun Caner (Eugene, OR: Harvest House, 2008), 40.

76. E.g., Georg Wilhelm Friedrich Hegel, *Lectures on the Philosophy of World History*, trans. H. B. Nisbet (Cambridge: Cambridge University Press, 1981), 17, 22.

77. E.g., G. W. F. Hegel, *The Phenomenology of Mind*, 2nd. ed., trans. J. B. Baillie (New York: Macmillan, 1931), 75.

this historicist approach to philosophical ideas features prominently in his apologetic method as well. *How Should We Then Live?* is a typical example, though in this work he seems to shy away from explicitly using Hegelian terms. In some of his other works, however, he frequently borrows the historicist language of Hegelian idealism. In *The Great Evangelical Disaster*, for example, he repeatedly cautions against the temptation to conform to the "world spirit of the age."[78]

The examples of Schaeffer, Van Til, Vos, and Bavinck show that the terminology and thought-form of Hegelian philosophy/philosophies can serve as effective instruments for communicating Christian-theistic worldviews to public spheres outside the church. This is, of course, not to identify these Reformed thinkers as Hegelians. They do not even belong to an idealist tradition. Yet they do remind us not to be afraid to use Hegel's insights for apologetic purposes, sometimes for the sake of engaging polemically with Hegelian idealism itself.

Learning from Hegel and Van Til: Method, Content, and Classical Theism

The way Bavinck, Vos, Van Til, and Schaeffer utilize aspects of Hegel's philosophical method without adopting its ontological content sheds light on an important topic in contemporary theology, namely, the interrelatedness between method and content. In modern times, it was Hegel who invented and propagated the notion that philosophical method and content are identical. This contention, as we saw in chapter 2, is based on the ontological assumption that human consciousness is ultimately identical with the mind of the absolute, and that the logic regulating human consciousness is identical with spirit. Reformed theologians like

---

78. Francis Schaeffer, *The Great Evangelical Disaster* (Wheaton, IL: Crossway, 1984), 23, 37–40, 101, 111.

Kuyper, Bavinck, Vos, and Van Til have rejected this ontology of divine-human identity and with it the identification of method and content. However, they have also been reminded by Hegel that no philosophical method is neutral: philosophical methods are developed upon the presuppositions of one's worldview.

In the twentieth century, Van Til's treatment of the relations between method and content is among the most thorough and faithful articulations of the basic principles of Reformed orthodoxy. In a nutshell, having rejected Hegel's identification between method and content, while having been reminded of their presuppositional interdependence, Van Til explains the relations between them in the patterns of *abiding distinction* and *inseparable unity*. Because of the inseparable unity, he does not adopt Hegelian methodology or that of any other non-Christian system wholesale. However, the abiding distinction enables him to utilize methodological aspects of Hegel's philosophy without adopting its ontological features.

The connection between method and content, according to Van Til, lies in the fundamental presupposition(s), or "starting point," of a philosophical system.[79] Method and content are to be viewed "as a whole" because they are rooted in the same starting point.[80] This view of method and content reflects the basic principles of the Reformed system. However, this must not be misunderstood to mean that we should reject all non-Christian methods so thoroughly that our own apologetic and theological methods contain no element or trace of them.

This serves as an important corrective to the modern and, I suspect, post-Hegelian myth that some methods must be completely rejected because of their underlying ontological assumptions. Hegel himself does not do this, to be sure, but the

---

79. Cornelius Van Til, *Christian Apologetics*, ed. William Edgar (Phillipsburg, NJ: P&R Publishing, 2003), 123.
80. Ibid., 123–24.

identification of logic and ontology, method and content, in a variety of sectors of philosophy and theology did in fact arise from him.

In modern and recent theology, the "scholastic" method of old, be it that of medieval Catholicism or Reformed orthodoxy, is often seen as antithetical to the Christian faith. Some Barthians, for example, think of scholasticism as a synonym of natural theology, which Barth famously calls an "invention of the Antichrist."[81] The same contention has come from many different sectors of contemporary theology that advocate the "de-Hellenization" of Christianity. They claim that "scholastic methods" must be rejected wholesale because they are inseparable from the basically Platonic presuppositions of Aristotelian metaphysics.[82] Some would even go so far as to claim that we should redefine or even give up some central tenets of classical

---

81. Karl Barth, *Church Dogmatics* I/1, ed. G. W. Bromiley and T. F. Torrance, trans. G. W. Bromiley (Edinburgh: T&T Clark, 1956), xiii.

82. The terms "Platonic" and "Platonist" are sometimes used interchangeably, but when we apply them to the history of philosophy, we have to understand their differences with reference to specific periods. While "Platonic" refers generally to philosophical traditions or themes that follow Plato's teachings, "Platonist" is a much more technical term. For example, against those who hold to the "entirely false" understanding that Plotinus was only reliant upon aspects of Plato's thought, but was not a Platonist (falsely defined as a follower of Plato) himself, Stephen Menn explains that "Plotinus was a Platonist, and to be a Platonist in the third century A.D. meant something definite: it meant to be a member of a certain school or *hairesis*. When in the year A.D. 176 the emperor Marcus Aurelius established four chairs of philosophy in Athens, he assigned one to the Epicureans, one to the Stoics, one to the Peripatetics, and one to the Platonists" (*Descartes and Augustine* [Cambridge: Cambridge University Press, 1998], 83). Thus, it would be inaccurate to say that the Peripatetics were Platonists. However, many scholars have acknowledged that Peripatetic/Aristotelian philosophy has a *Platonic* core. Archie Spencer, for instance, rightly points out that both Aristotle's "theory of analogy and the net result of his *Metaphysics* . . . remain essentially Platonic" in prioritizing "suprasensible" forms. He astutely observes that at the core of this association of form and substance is what he calls the Platonic principle of "cause-effect resemblance" (*The Analogy of Faith: The Quest for God's Speakability* [Downers Grove, IL: IVP Academic, 2015], 40).

theism, such as divine impassibility and immutability, and see change and suffering as having really occurred within some aspect of God's being.

Van Til is also known for his staunch opposition to the natural theology of medieval scholasticism. Just as he is not afraid to adopt aspects of Hegel's philosophical method, however, he never fully jettisoned the scholastic method that Reformed orthodoxy critically appropriated from medieval and classical philosophy. Van Til's doctrine of God, which lies at the core of his Christian worldview, relies heavily on historic Reformed orthodoxy, which adopted a method often referred to as "scholastic." When he speaks of "the unity of God," for instance, Van Til follows Reformed orthodoxy in distinguishing "between the unity of singularity (*singularitatis*) and the unity of simplicity (*simplicitatis*)."[83] He defines the "unity of singularity" as "numerical oneness," a concept derived from the Aristotelian distinction between *numerical* and *specific unities*.

The numerical-specific distinction in the Reformed doctrine of God is a classic instance in which Reformed orthodox theologians explicitly appeal to Aristotelian *logic* despite their rejection of Aristotelian *metaphysics*. In *Categories*, the first of his six works on logic, Aristotle identifies ten categories in which an object is apprehended by the human mind.[84] The first of these is *substance*. Aristotle distinguishes between primary and secondary substances. A primary substance is an individual *qua* individual—the particular as opposed to the universal. A secondary substance, by contrast, refers to the universal and is defined in terms of forms and natures. So, for instance, "Socrates" is a primary substance, while "mankind" is the secondary substance to which the former pertains. As primary substances, Socrates and Plato are *numerically*

83. Van Til, *Christian Apologetics*, 25.
84. See Aristotle, *Categories*, in *The Complete Works of Aristotle*, ed. Jonathan Barnes, trans. John Ackrill (Princeton, NJ: Princeton University Press, 2014).

distinct. Yet they pertain to the same human *species*, and so they are *specifically* one.

Reformed orthodox theologians of the seventeenth century adopted this logical (not metaphysical) distinction and applied it to a wide range of doctrinal topics. In sorting out the traducian-creationist debate, for instance, Reformed scholastics subscribed to the basic principle that human souls are numerically many and specifically one. When it comes to the doctrine of God, the same logical distinction is helpful in clarifying that the three persons of the Godhead are a unity both specifically and numerically.

In one sense, it is true that Van Til rejects the Aristotelian "method" of so-called scholastic theology. This may seem to complicate his intellectual relation to so-called Reformed scholasticism. We must understand, however, that the term "method" can be equivocal, and writers commenting on Van Til's thought have not always been clear about what particular aspect of scholastic "method" he rejects.

In modern and contemporary scholarship, the term "metaphysics" refers both to the substantive content of this branch of philosophy and to the methodology it entails. "Scholasticism," then, is often understood as having appealed to the method of Aristotelian metaphysics. Interpretation of reality in terms of *causation*, for example, is a fundamental aspect of this method. While it is true that medieval scholasticism embraced this metaphysical method and developed an elaborate system on this basis, the same is hardly the case with Reformed orthodoxy.

At this juncture, we must distinguish between the *logical* and the *metaphysical* aspects of what modern and contemporary scholars call "Aristotelian method." On the Peripatetic understanding, the method and content of philosophy are strictly distinct: Aristotelian *logic* constitutes the *method* of philosophy, but is not itself a branch of philosophy. What the Peripatetics did not realize was that Aristotelian *metaphysics* is part and parcel of what moderns have recognized as its *metaphysical method*. This means that the philosophical method that Aristotle and his followers employed is not restricted to his logic. Apart from his logic, there is a metaphysical aspect to his method that is basically inseparable from his overall philosophical system.

However, we must also understand that the method that Aristotle lays down in his six works on logic, to which the Peripatetics gave the name *Organon*, is not nearly as interwoven with the substantive content of his philosophy as with his metaphysical method. In contrast to the metaphysical aspect, the logical aspect of Aristotle's method can be much more easily detached from the presuppositions of his philosophical system and applied to a different system with entirely different presuppositions.

What sets Reformed orthodoxy apart from medieval scholasticism, especially that of the Thomistic school, is the former's rejection of Aristotelian metaphysics and the natural theology to which it gave rise. As Calvin and Reformed theologians of the orthodox period see it, the Thomistic-Aristotelian construal of God in relation to the world in terms of the central metaphysical notion of *causality* inevitably wipes out the Creator-creature distinction that lies at the very foundation of Christian theology. It is true that Calvin and later Reformed orthodoxy adopted the Aristotelian language of causality, but, in so doing, their purpose was highly polemical. They firmly rejected the Thomistic-Aristotelian understanding of the divine causation of the world (this is a point to which we shall return).

In this particular sense, we can say that Reformed orthodoxy refused to adopt the Aristotelian method of medieval scholasticism. What this means, however, is that Reformed scholasticism rejected the *metaphysical* aspect of Aristotelian method. Yet the *logical* aspect of Aristotelian method can, for the most part, be abstracted from the substantive content of Aristotle's philosophy and critically applied to the Christian project of *fides quaerens intellectum*. The numerical-specific distinction is one of many examples of the Reformed appropriation of the *logical* aspect of Aristotelian method.

Van Til is not afraid to follow his Reformed predecessors in utilizing this aspect of Aristotelian method, just as he does not shy away from using elements of Hegel's method. For Van Til, the method is distinct, albeit inseparable, from the content, and so elements of a method can be abstracted from its system—the sunken treasures can and should be salvaged from the shipwreck and brought back to the house of God from which they were originally taken.

Van Til provides an important corrective to contemporary theologians who propose to renounce "scholasticism" and classical theism. The fact is that more often than not one originally non-Christian method is substituted for another: Hegelian thought is often unwittingly introduced to outweigh the allegedly Platonic and/or Aristotelian elements of classical theism.

One of my hopes in writing this book is that the reader, having become acquainted with Hegel's philosophy, will be able to discern traces of his influence in the writings of those theologians who attribute process to the being of God. Jürgen Moltmann and Wolfhart Pannenberg are typical examples in recent theology. In contemporary English-language Barth studies, some have attempted to rid Barthian theology of every last vestige of traditional metaphysics by denouncing the substantialism of classical theism and replacing it with the view that the act of divine election constitutes God's triune being.[85] Against these highly Hegelian tendencies, Van Til provides a reminder

---

85. This view was first expounded by Bruce McCormack and has been championed by Paul Nimmo, Paul Dafydd Jones, and Matthias Gockel, among others. While McCormack expressed this view early in his career, it was his *Cambridge Companion* chapter that brought this controversial view into the spotlight. See Bruce

for Reformed believers that the Christian doctrine of God should not be reduced to a choice between Platonic idealism and Hegelian idealism.

It is true that orthodox theology, which subscribes to classical theism, sees the Son of God as having really suffered and really died a *human death* in his very *person*. It was not the human *nature* of Christ that died, for natures are predicates/forms and not subjects. Persons are the subjects of their deaths, not natures. The person of Christ is the agent and subject of all his experiences and activities, including suffering and death. This person is none other than the second person of the triune God. Hence, the Reformed confession of the "death of the Son of God" (Canons of Dort, II.3). To assert that it was not the Son of God, but rather the man Jesus, who died would be tantamount to committing the heresy of Nestorianism (one to which Nestorius himself did not subscribe), namely, the fatal error of splitting Christ into two persons.

Yet precisely here we need to add at once that the immortal Son died without ceasing to be immortal. The Son's real experience of human suffering and death is an addition to his divine person *qua* God. The Son "emptied" himself (Phil. 2:7), not by *losing* anything in his divine person and being, but by *adding* a creaturely nature to his divine person that remained without change and without confusion with his human nature in the union of the two. Whatever changes, losses, and sufferings the Son underwent, he underwent strictly according to his human nature, while his whole divine person in his divine nature never ceased to be impassible, immutable, and immortal.

The sufferings and death of Christ caused no change or loss in the being of God—not even his immanent "existence in time," as some have claimed. Even before the incarnation, God's

---

McCormack, "Grace and Being: the Role of God's Gracious Election in Karl Barth's Theological Ontology," in *The Cambridge Companion to Karl Barth*, ed. John Webster (Cambridge: Cambridge University Press, 2000), 127–42.

temporal economy in the creaturely world must be understood as works *additional* and *external* (*ad extra*) to his being. We must never attribute any process to the being of God, for that would put us on a slippery slope towards Hegelian idealism. Nor should we ever ascribe two modes of existence to God's being, claiming on the one hand that God in his transcendent and eternal nature cannot change or suffer, and on the other hand that God's being really changes and suffers in his temporal mode of existence. This would be tantamount to a split in the Godhead.

We noted earlier that Reformed theology, more than any other brand of Christianity, emphasizes the abiding distinction between Christ's two natures. This is part and parcel of the Reformed insistence upon the Creator-creature distinction, the very doctrine that makes us immune to Hegel's philosophy of divine-human identity. As Reformed Christians, we must stress that God the Son was really afflicted with transience, suffering, and death only in the sense that these experiences really pertained to the creaturely nature appended to his person (though we must also recognized that the Son's assumption of human nature makes his person fully and truly human). The same pattern of thinking also applies to God's temporal interactions with creatures before the incarnation. These temporal works, we stress again, are *ad extra* to God's being, which cannot be split into two modes of existence. Attributing different modes of existence—different moments—to the divine being is almost characteristically Hegelian. The immanent Trinity and economic Trinity are not two moments of God's being. They are rather the distinction between God's *being ad intra* and God's *acts and works ad extra*.

Here it may be helpful to introduce a logical distinction in Latin scholastic theology: *secundum quid* and *simpliciter*. *Secundum quid* refers to the contingency of a truth-claim upon the validity of certain preconditions, while *simpliciter* means that a proposition is true on its own terms. The statement "Hegel was born in Germany," for example, is true only *secundum quid*. In Hegel's time, Germany did not exist as a unified nation or state. We can say that he was born in Germany only in the sense that the city in which he was born was to become part of modern-day Germany. So, Hegel was *simpliciter* born in Stuttgart, and *secundum quid* born in Germany.

This distinction helps us to wrap our minds around the truth of the statement that the person—the whole person—of the Son really suffered and died. This statement is not true *simpliciter*, but is true *secundum quid*. The truth value of this proposition hinges upon the Son's assumption of human nature, an event contingent upon God's free decision that is in no sense necessitated by his nature. God is *simpliciter* triune, *simpliciter* love, *simpliciter* righteous, and *simpliciter* all that he is. But God the Son suffered and died *secundum quid*: the Son in his necessarily divine nature never suffered and never died, but because the whole person *became* fully and truly human, we can say that the Son really became corruptible and mortal. The death of Christ was *simpliciter* the death of a man and *secundum quid*, by virtue of the unity of his person, the death of the immortal Son who never ceased to be immortal.

Attributing suffering and transience to the nature of God *simpliciter*, without acknowledging the abiding distinction between the Creator and his creation, and the abiding distinction between Christ's two natures as a corollary of it, inevitably opens up a Pandora's box of Hegelian ontology. It leads to a slippery slope towards process theology of various sorts. It introduces what Van Til aptly calls a "split in the Godhead" after Hegel (as we saw earlier): we end up with a divine mode of existence in which God's immanent nature is mutable and passible, separate from his atemporal and immutable mode of existence, in which his "transcendent nature," on post-Kantian and post-Hegelian assumptions, is inevitably rendered unknowable to human reason.[86] Here we stress once more that a firm grasp of the Reformed formulation of the Creator-creature distinction, including its corollary of two-nature Christology, is the antidote that makes us immune to Hegelianism.

Reformed Criticisms of Hegel

A Rationalism Unavoidably Irrationalistic

The previous section has alluded to how Reformed theologians have rejected Hegel's philosophy of divine-human identity. This rejection follows naturally from the obvious fact that his monistic worldview is fundamentally incompatible with the Christian faith. Faith, however, finds its joy in reasoned understanding. The theologian's intellect is not content in merely rejecting Hegel's worldview on the basis of faith. We need to offer a reasoned refutation of its presuppositions in defense of our own.

In this section, we shall rely on Bavinck and Van Til to disclose the self-contradictory implications of fundamental Hegelian presuppositions. The thrust of their criticism is that Hegel's "monistic assumptions" inevitably lead to what Van Til calls "irrationalism."[87] This unavoidable result, of course, contradicts the core intention of Hegel's philosophy. Bavinck rightly points out that "Hegel's goal" is to "reconcile" faith and reason.[88] In Hegel's rational idealism, "the Cartesian premise finds its ultimate expression": "thinking produces being; all being, accordingly, is logical, rational."[89]

On Hegel's "monistic assumptions," Van Til comments, "unless man can *exhaustively* reduce all factual historical existence

---

86. Van Til, *Systematic Theology*, 323.
87. Ibid., 291.
88. Bavinck, *Reformed Dogmatics*, 1:166.
89. Ibid.

to changeless logical relations, there is that which is utterly undetermined and unknowable."[90] This criterion of rationality is one that Hegel himself fails to meet. Van Til appeals to Søren Kierkegaard's criticism of Hegel to argue that "by seeking to show by logical manipulation how all reality must be what it is," Hegel "kills all uniqueness and all genuine newness in history."[91] This is a point that we already explained when we discussed Hegel's monistic understanding of the concrete universal: contra his own intentions, his identification of human consciousness with spirit ultimately annihilates particularity and concretion.

Yet the problems of Hegel's monism run deeper than that. Van Til takes note of the critical-Kantian core of the philosopher's thought. He observes that Hegel "does not believe in the idea of God as a constitutive concept. For him the idea of a god is a limiting concept."[92] Recall from chapter 2 that the Kantian notion of a constitutive concept, simply put, denotes an object of which an actual existence-claim is made. A limiting concept, by contrast, is an idea postulated for the explanation of observable phenomena. Kant treats God as a constitutive principle only in the realm of practical reason, but as far as pure theoretical reason is concerned, God is merely a postulate. What Van Til means here is that Hegel's phenomenological method is in line with Kant's critique of theoretical reason: Hegel does not acknowledge the objective existence of God as a being over against the world of historical phenomena. Hegel's god is postulated only to explicate the purposiveness of history, the universality and particularity of being, and so on.

---

90. Van Til, *Systematic Theology*, 290. Emphasis added. Here Van Til is engaging one of his contemporary critics and opponents, J. Oliver Buswell.

91. Ibid. Van Til rejects what he perceives to be Kierkegaard's argument against Hegel. Few Kierkegaard scholars today would agree with Van Til's interpretation of the Danish philosopher.

92. Ibid., 291.

Van Til explains that Hegel's "idea of the limiting concept is based on the monist assumption that unless man can himself logicize reality, that is, show how all factual existence is reducible to loci in a network of logical relations, to that extent reality is irrational."[93] According to Hegel, human beings can logicize reality only because human consciousness is ultimately identical with the divine, "for if all reality is of one piece . . . , then the human mind and the divine mind are also of one piece. The divine mind does not then know anything more, and the divine will does not then control anything more, than does the human mind and the human will."[94] Because the universe remains mysterious to the human mind, it remains mysterious to the divine mind also. The divine mind does not know itself exhaustively, and, by virtue of the divine-human identification, the human mind can know neither itself nor the logic of the universe (that is, the divine mind) exhaustively. Thus, Hegel cannot escape the unintended conclusion that "reality is ultimately mysterious."[95] Despite his rationalist attempt to logically systemize the truth of the universe, then, he becomes on his own terms an irrationalist.

An Idealism Unavoidably Materialistic

Before we return to the topic of Hegel's inevitably irrationalistic rationalism, we may observe here that in many ways he can be appreciated as reacting against the Platonist (and not just Platonic) notion of God that has served as both an inspiration and a grave challenge to major Christian traditions since the period of the early church.[96] The Platonist god, called "the One"

93. Ibid.
94. Ibid., 292.
95. Ibid.
96. Platonist cosmogony, mainly based on sometimes forced interpretations of Plato's *Timaeus*, is in fact highly organicist. Plato himself visualized the universe as a

or "the Good," is absolutely immutable and simple. Its absolute simplicity means that the Good/the One does not pertain to the realm of beings. That is, we cannot say that the Good/the One "is" this or that, for this would posit a subject-predicate distinction within it and destroy its simplicity. It does not admit predications. Its simplicity means that it is indescribable and therefore unknowable. It cannot even possess self-knowledge, for the act of knowing presupposes an object, and a subject-object distinction within the Good/the One would also imply a denial of its absolute simplicity. Moreover, the Good/the One is absolutely eternal and immutable, and the act of knowing, just as any activity, presupposes change. Thus, the Good/the One cannot be known and cannot know itself.[97]

Historic proponents of what Bavinck and Van Til call "orthodox theology," such as Anselm, have critically—very critically—appropriated and recalibrated the Platonist notions of divine immutability and simplicity, and incorporated them in the biblical understanding of divine transcendence.[98] For a long time in the history of Western Christianity, mainstream thinkers have taken for granted that the transcendent and therefore incomprehensible God is knowable to human reason through revelation. Even many philosophers who rejected the orthodox view of revelation assumed that innate ideas, innate knowledge, and/or sensory data are trustworthy because they were ordained by

---

living organism. The Platonist creator, the Demiurge, is also described as a conscious living thing, capable of activity. The Good/the One, however, is absolutely simple and immutable, and no inner life process can be attributed to it.

97. For more details, see Eyjólfur Emilsson, *Plotinus on Intellect* (Oxford: Oxford University Press, 2007), 1–5.

98. Bavinck offers an account of the early Christian appropriation and transformation of the "Platonic" notion of divine simplicity in *Reformed Dogmatics*, 2:118. Sometimes this transformation involved complete redefinitions of key philosophical terms like *hypostases*. See John Zizioulas, "Human Capacity and Human Incapacity: A Theological Exploration of Personhood," *Scottish Journal of Theology* 28 (1975): 409.

God. Yet from the time of Kant onward, the originally Platonist notion of divine transcendence began to make a comeback in a modern form, and, as Bavinck observes, "the doctrine of the unknowability of God has progressively penetrated modern consciousness."[99]

Following Kant, mainline philosophers like Fichte typically associated *rational unknowability* with divine transcendence. The post-Kantian impulse in Hegel also dictates that transcendence goes hand in hand with unknowability. To establish divine knowability, Hegel thought that it was necessary to deny divine transcendence as originally defined in Platonist terms.

Hegel's strategy, as we have seen, was to modernize Aristotle's philosophy by reinterpreting substance as living subject. As early as the *Phenomenology of Spirit,* Hegel saw in Aristotle a latent philosophy of divine-human identity. Aristotle identifies God as the Unmoved Mover, who brings every substance into existence. Hegel sees in Aristotelian theology a divine being who is self-moved and who is knowable through nature, since the whole of nature is the divine being's very own purposive activity.[100] In Aristotelian ontology, the divine can really be called a being; predications can be made about it; nature can be understood in light of it.

From a Reformed perspective, if the problem with Aristotelian theology is that it effectively discards all adequate notions of transcendence by seeing the divine as ontologically connected to nature through causation, the problem with Hegel's system is that it pushes the divine-human connection in Aristotle to its logical extreme. Hegel's god is not merely an Unmoved Mover; it is movement itself. In Hegel, the divine is wholly identified with nature, and the mind of the natural universe is wholly identified

---

99. Bavinck, *Reformed Dogmatics,* 2:43.
100. Hegel, *Phenomenology,* 83.

with the consciousness of the human species. Because Hegel identifies human beings as spirit, he considers himself an idealist.

But what are the implications of this monistic idealism? Rather than looking into Hegel's own writings and drawing out its implications, Bavinck beats Hegel in his own game by tracing the historical development of his thought. Bavinck acknowledges that initially many "right wing" (referring to the Right Hegelians, also known as Old Hegelians or the Hegelian Right) scholars found promise in Hegel's "reconciliation of theology and philosophy."[101] Bavinck does not deny that there is a great deal that Christian theologians can learn from Hegel. Yet Bavinck points out that Hegel's presupposition of ultimate divine-human identity, which lies at the heart of his reconciliation of theology and philosophy, inevitably implies the annihilation of the essence of theology *qua theo*-logy.

This "became clear," Bavinck observes, very soon in the generation of Ludwig Feuerbach (1804–72) and David Friedrich Strauss (1808–74).[102] It is certainly not merely incidental that Feuerbach and Strauss, like Hegel, both started out as students of Christian theology. Both Feuerbach and Strauss studied at the University of Berlin, where Hegel was once the chair of the philosophy department. Feuerbach began as a student at Heidelberg and later moved to Berlin in order to study with Hegel. Strauss gave up a seminary professorship and enrolled as a student at Berlin, arriving in the autumn of 1831 shortly after an outbreak of cholera had subsided. Upon his first meeting with Friedrich Schleiermacher, the master asked him whether he had heard that Hegel had just died on the previous day. Strauss blurted out, "But it was for his sake that I came here to Berlin!"[103]

---

101. Bavinck, *Reformed Dogmatics*, 1:166.
102. Ibid.
103. Horton Harris, *David Friedrich Strauss and His Theology* (Cambridge: Cambridge University Press, 1974), 29.

The implications that Feuerbach and Strauss drew from Hegel were so significant that the twentieth-century theologian Karl Barth would come to remark rather famously: "Proper theology begins just at the point where the difficulties disclosed by Strauss and Feuerbach are seen and then laughed at."[104] This is an insight that Bavinck would very well agree with.

Simply put, Bavinck observes, Feuerbach and Strauss both took Hegel's position that "God and man are one" to its logical end, and "both Feuerbach and Strauss ended up in materialism: sensual nature is the only reality; human beings are what they eat."[105] The two former Berlin students demonstrated that the monistic and panentheistic core of Hegel's idealism inevitably leads to materialism.

In *The Essence of Christianity*, Feuerbach appeals to Hegel's divine-human identification to argue that the essence of theology is in fact anthropology. What Feuerbach means is that "God" is nothing but humankind's consciousness of the infinitude of its own nature. Despite Hegel's persistent contention for the knowability and objectivity of God, the subject-object identification in Hegel's concept of reconciliation provides Feuerbach with a way to flip Hegel on his head, as it were, claiming that the essence of religion is human self-projection onto a pseudo-object: "In the consciousness of the infinite, the conscious [human] subject has for his object the infinity of his own nature."[106]

For Hegel, the pure concept that Christianity as the consummate religion represents is the manifestation of spirit. According to his idealism, *human beings are spirit*. Feuerbach does little more than simply flip the very same coin upside down, turning the

---

104. Karl Barth, *Protestant Theology in the Nineteenth Century*, trans. Brian Cozens and John Bowden (Grand Rapids: Eerdmans, 2002), 554.
105. Bavinck, *Reformed Dogmatics*, 1:256.
106. Ludwig Feuerbach, *The Essence of Christianity*, trans. George Eliot (New York: Prometheus, 1989), 2–3.

subject-predicate relation around to assert that *spirit is human.* For both of them, spirit has no objective existence apart from subjective human individuals. Feuerbach convincingly shows that on this view, the essence of religion is but human self-projection; God is the mirror of humankind; religious consciousness is not the consciousness of an objectively real God, but of human self-consciousness; the essence of religion is idolatry, and the essence of theology is anthropology. That is, the God of whom Christians speak is but an idol that theologians created in their own image.

Hegel's arguments for divine-human identity ultimately lead to Feuerbach's conclusion:

> Religion, at least the Christian, is the relation of man to himself, or more correctly to his own nature (i.e., his subjective nature).... The divine being is nothing else than the human being, or rather, the human nature purified, freed from the limits of the individual man, made objective—i.e., contemplated and revered as another.... All the attributes of the divine nature are ... attributes of the human nature.[107]

Strauss's thought was more nuanced than Feuerbach's in that the former sought to do much more than simply develop the implications of Hegel's system. In fact, Strauss eventually came to be denounced by the Left Hegelians led by Bruno Bauer, who argued that Strauss actually derived his ideas from Schleiermacher, rather than Hegel. In 1838, Strauss admitted that he was inspired by neither Hegel's theology nor his philosophy, and broke with the Left Hegelians thereafter.

Still, if we consider his monumental *Life of Jesus, Critically Examined,* we would find strong Hegelian elements in it—not least Hegel's central notion of divine-human identification. This

---

107. Ibid., 14.

controversial opus challenges the historicity of the miracles reported in the Gospels, and alleges that the Bible should be read and appreciated as *mythus*, the value of which lies not in the historicity of the events that it claims to report, but in the *concept*, the pure truth, that the historically incredible tales aim to convey. The true concept of the Bible is unearthed only by the method of *demythologization*.

This method resonates deeply with the Hegelian distinction between representation (*Vorstellung*) and concept (*Begriff*). Strauss borrows Hegelian terminology to define *mythus* as "the representation of an event or of an idea in a form which is historical, but, at the same time characterized by the rich pictorial and imaginative mode of thought and expression of the primitive ages."[108]

At the beginning of *The Life of Jesus*, Strauss sounds very much like a deist who believes in a transcendent and unknowable Creator: "God operates on the world only in so far as he gave to it this fixed direction at the creation. From this point of view, at which nature and history appear as a compact tissue of finite causes and effects, it was impossible to regard the narratives of the Bible, in which this tissue is broken by innumerable instances of divine interference, as historical."[109] It soon becomes clear, however, that the "God" of whom Strauss speaks is not even a deistic one that exists objectively apart from the world.

Bavinck rightly points out that Strauss's notion of divinity is basically Hegelian: it is "the eternal process that produces the world from within itself, and only comes to self-consciousness, personality, and itself in humanity."[110] This Hegelian understanding of divine-human identity is, as Strauss himself puts it,

---

108. David Strauss, *The Life of Jesus Critically Examined*, trans. George Eliot, 3 vols. (London: Continuum, 2005), 3:28.

109. Ibid., 1:59–60.

110. Bavinck, *Reformed Dogmatics*, 1:256.

"the absolute sense of Christology," the concept underneath the mythical representation of the Gospels.[111] For Strauss, "the key to the whole of Christology" lies in the idea of the unity of the human and the divine, not in an individual human being (i.e., Jesus), but in the species (at this point Strauss and Feuerbach converge).[112] "In an individual, a God-man, the properties and functions which the church ascribed to Christ contradict themselves; in the idea of the race, they perfectly agree. Humanity is the union of the two natures—God become man, the infinite manifesting itself in the finite, and the finite spirit remembering its infinitude."[113] Bavinck summarizes Strauss's view: "Strauss . . . held that the infinite pours itself out in the finite, not, however, in the individual person but in humanity as a whole. Humanity is the true son of God, the ideal Christ."[114]

Bavinck aptly observes that, according to Strauss, the claims that "God and man are one" and that "humanity is the true son of God" imply that "all miracles are excluded."[115] Strauss, like Feuerbach, ended up as a materialist. What Feuerbach and Strauss have disclosed is that the Hegelian god is really not a supernatural being at all. In identifying the divine with the natural, Hegel's idealism is really materialism in disguise. The theology of which the philosopher comes to the rescue is but anthropology in disguise. The Hegelian god has no consciousness of its own apart from the collective consciousness of the human species, and this means that the mental process of the divine is naturalistic through and through.

Hegel is well aware that the mind of God is what gives purpose and meaning to the universe. The consciousness of the

---

111. Strauss, *Life of Jesus*, 3:348.
112. Ibid.
113. Ibid., 3:435–36.
114. Bavinck, *Reformed Dogmatics*, 1:166.
115. Ibid., 1:256.

absolute is what guarantees the purposiveness of individual human minds. Without the divine mind, world history that consists of the development of collective human consciousness would be completely random and irrationalistic. This is precisely why Hegel appeals to the divine mind as the concrete universal. Hegel's intention is to identify nature as God's purposive activity. To that end, he comes to the aid of the Christian religion by subjugating it to his philosophical system.

The unintended result, however, is that the essence of religion is rendered idolatry. Divine activity is reduced to natural causation and process. God has no existence except in the form of human consciousness, which means that God has no real existence at all. Feuerbach and Strauss, as Bavinck points out, have disclosed to us that Hegel finally failed to find the divine plan for the universal that he initially set out to look for. Hegel has only nature to look to. There is ultimately no God and therefore no concrete universal in Hegel's system. According to the rules of his own game, this means that genuine human knowledge of reality, meaning, and purpose is ultimately impossible, and that reality is irrational. This leads us back to Van Til's charge of irrationalism: Hegel's system is unable to render genuine rational knowledge of reality. Later dialectical materialists would argue that the Hegelian understanding of history as purposive activity is compatible with materialism, but Hegel himself knew better: without God as the concrete universal, even the fairest universe would appear to human understanding as nothing more than what the ancient Greek philosopher Heraclitus famously described as "a heap of rubbish piled up at random." Despite his own rationalistic idealist intentions, this irrational materialism is the worldview that Hegel's monistic presuppositions ultimately lead to.

Conclusion: A Christian Answer to Hegel

Having offered the foregoing criticisms, we must remind ourselves that disclosing the contradictions in, and failures of, Hegel's system should not be an end in itself. If we cannot provide an answer that brings hope to people and glory to God, all our criticisms would be but resounding gongs and clanging cymbals.

To pick up where we left off in the last section, let us begin with the notion of divine transcendence. A true and adequate understanding of divine transcendence, as has been recognized in Western philosophy since the time of Plato, requires two basic elements. First, in relation to the creaturely universe, God's transcendence is defined in terms of an ontological divide between the created and the uncreated. Second, in and of himself, God is eternal, self-existent, immutable, impassible, and simple. These basic conceptual requirements are acknowledged even by Strauss.[116]

Let us begin with the ontological divide between the created and the uncreated. In Christian theology, this divide takes on the form of the Creator-creature distinction. As we have seen, Reformed theology places a strong emphasis on this distinction, probably more so than any other major orthodox theological tradition. This is what made Reformed theologians like Bavinck and Van Til immune to Hegel's panentheistic monism as they appropriated formal aspects of Hegelian thought without adopting its substantive contents.

In the Western branches of Christianity, the dominant paradigm for understanding the biblical doctrine of the Creator-creature distinction came from Augustine. On the basis of the biblical doctrine of God's creation of the universe out of nothing

---

116. Strauss, *Life of Jesus*, 1:58.

(*creatio ex nihilo*), Augustine constructed an elaborate ontology covering a wide range of profound questions regarding form and matter, soul and body, the image of God in human beings and Christ as the image of God, the cause of evil and what it is or what it is not, etc. How much of this ontology was based on sound exegesis and how much of it was derived from Greek philosophy has been a subject of intense debate for almost a century.[117] Even scholars who avidly emphasize Augustine's

---

117. In the 1930s, a number of European scholars presented convincing evidence of Augustine's heavy reliance on the Platonist thinkers of his time. See Willy Theiler, *Porphyrios und Augustin* (Halle: Niemeyer, 1933); Paul Henry, *Plotin et l'Occident* (Louvain: Spicilegium Sacrum Lovaniense, 1934). One well-established paradigm even identifies Augustine as a "Christian Platonist": see Philip Cary, *Augustine's Invention of the Inner Self: The Legacy of a Christian Platonist* (Oxford: Oxford University Press, 2003). On the other hand, G. L. Prestige and his followers hold to the so-called "Greek-Latin dichotomy" paradigm and argue that Augustine's ontology is significantly different from that of the classical philosophers and even the Greek Fathers, because his Latin intellect and language were incapable of capturing the subtleties of Greek ontology. See G. L. Prestige, *God in Patristic Thought* (London: SPCK, 1959). But Robert O'Connell, one of the most authoritative readers of Augustine in recent decades, has demonstrated the Latin Father's familiarity with Greek metaphysics and argues that at some of the most important junctures of his writings, the theologian failed to carry through with his intention to honor his basic Christian convictions and resist the influence of Platonist philosophy. In like manner, J. M. Rist argues that in some important aspects of his theology, Augustine is more devoted to Platonist philosophy than to his biblical view of *creatio ex nihilo*. See Robert O' Connell, *The Origin of the Soul in St. Augustine's Later Works* (New York: Fordham University Press, 1987); J. M. Rist, *Augustine: Ancient Thought Baptized* (Cambridge: Cambridge University Press, 1994). Scholars like Stephen Menn, who emphasize that "Augustine was not a Platonist," also admit that "to a great extent" Augustine's concepts and doctrines are "the same as Plotinus's concepts and doctrines" (Menn, *Descartes and Augustine*, 144). Other scholars, such as Gillian Evans, Carol Harrison, Janet Soskice, and, more recently, Gerald Boersma, tend to stress Augustine's basic opposition to Platonist ontology, but even they would still admit that the Latin theologian retained important aspects of Platonism. See Gillian Evans, *Augustine on Evil* (Cambridge: Cambridge University Press, 1990); Carol Harrison, *Beauty and Revelation in the Thought of Augustine* (Oxford: Clarendon Press, 1992); Janet Soskice, "Augustine on Knowing God and Knowing the Self," in *Faithful Reading: New Essays in Theology in Honour of Fergus Kerr, O.P.*, ed. T. O'Loughlin, K. Kilby, and S. Oliver (London: T&T Clark, 2012); Gerald Boersma, *Augustine's*

opposition to Greek philosophy, however, would still admit that some features of his ontology came from Platonism and other classical sources.[118] In due course, as we shall see, Calvin and later Reformed theologians would offer critical corrections of the remaining pagan elements in Augustine's thought.[119] The basic structure of Augustine's ontology, grounded on the doctrine of *creatio ex nihilo*, summarized as follows, has nevertheless been adopted as the orthodox norm of Reformed theology:

(1) The triune God is self-existent in his intra-Trinitarian (*ad intra*) relations.
(2) Everything other than God came into being, not by itself, but by God's creation. God created the entire universe out of nothing in one single act of original creation.
(3) God is the Creator, and everything other than God is a creature—hence, the Creator-creature distinction that underlies orthodox Christian theology.
(4) Ultimately there are only two kinds of beings: God, as eternal and self-existent being, or "Being Itself," and created beings, which were nothing before God created them.
(5) God is absolutely, supremely, and unchangeably good.
(6) Since the cause of the existence of all things is the goodness of the Creator, all created things are by nature good,

---

Early Theology of Image: A Study in the Development of Pro-Nicene Theology (Oxford: Oxford University Press, 2016).

118. Evans, for instance, argues that Plotinus's "*Enneads* contain a theory of evil which ... Augustine rejected as a whole," even though he "retained many of its parts." Evans, *Augustine on Evil*, 39.

119. One example is Augustine's meontological account of evil. Calvin does not entirely reject the Augustinian view of evil as *privatio boni*, but he finds this view inadequate, and devises a distinction between primary and secondary causality to honor the biblical passages indicating that God is actively at work when evil occurs. For more details, see Heath White, "Theological Determinism and the 'Authoring Sin' Objection," in *Calvinism and the Problem of Evil*, ed. David E. Alexander and Daniel M. Johnson (Eugene, OR: Pickwick, 2016).

though not unchangeably or absolutely so, but good only in accordance with their own kind or nature.

(7) There is not a third kind of substance that is neither God nor a created thing, since if something other than God were uncreated, it would have been self-existent as some kind of a second god alongside the one true God.

For Augustine, *creatio ex nihilo* goes hand in hand with his Christian understanding of divine transcendence. God is transcendent, "not in the way that oil floats on water, nor as heaven is above earth."[120] Rather, God is transcendent in that he is eternal and self-existent as the Creator, and that everything else is a creature that came into being from nothing through God's creation.[121]

This view of divine transcendence is more radical than even that of Platonism, which still maintains some sort of ontological connections between God and creatures through certain processes of emanations. The doctrine of *creatio ex nihilo* meant for Augustine that God and creatures are not ontologically connected. This became a significant challenge to Augustine, because he had to rationally explicate the biblical predication, *God is*, a predication that even the weaker view of transcendence espoused by Platonism forbade. Recall that the Platonist notion of immutability forbids that the transcendent Good be involved in any sort of activity. The Good/the One did not create the world; the Demiurge did, through an intermediary World-Soul. Moreover, the Platonist notion of transcendence entails an understanding of absolute unity and simplicity that defies any sort of *ad intra* differentiation. The Good as such cannot be identified as a being: it cannot even be itself or know

---

120. Augustine, *Confessions*, trans. Henry Chadwick (Oxford: Oxford University Press, 1991), 124.

121. Ibid.

itself, since self-being and self-knowledge presuppose self-differentiation.

Augustine's challenge was to speak of God as being while staying true to the biblical view of divine transcendence. The Thomistic-Aristotelian interpretation of the Mosaic name of God as being in the sense of uncaused first cause was not readily available to Augustine. Even if it was, Augustine did not appeal to Aristotle's authority the way Thomas did. Furthermore, this Aristotelian understanding contradicts Augustine's adherence to certain Platonist principles. As Menn puts it, "Augustine says that inferior things *are* because they are from God. St. Thomas might say the same; but Thomas would mean that God makes creatures actually exist by communicating the act of existence to essences that do not have existence of themselves."[122]

Augustine associates God with the Greek concept of "being," and tells us in *Confessions* 7.10.16 that this association is based on his exegesis of the divine name, "I am that I am." The problem here is how to reconcile the notion of divine transcendence, which entails, *inter alia*, the notion of simplicity, with this biblical name of God. Augustine accepts the Platonist understanding of the transcendence of the Good in terms of simplicity. The name "I am that I am," then, contradicts Augustine's understanding of transcendence. To uphold a genuine and adequate notion of divine transcendence, it seems that revelation would be impossible. A transcendent God could not possibly say to Moses, "I am that I am," without at once destroying his very own simplicity and immutability.

Hegel, as we have seen, was confronted with the very same problem, albeit in a modern form. His strategy to overcome the unknowability of God was to reduce the ontological Trinity to a logical trinity, and ascribe transcendence merely to the

---

122. Menn, *Descartes and Augustine*, 169.

first moment of logic, eventually to be sublated in the process of divine growth. In this way, Hegel also denied the Creator-creature distinction.

In Western theology since the time of Augustine, the orthodox doctrine of the Trinity has allowed us to attribute both diversity and simplicity to the one divine essence. As Augustine puts it, God is "a substance both simple and manifold."[123] In the final section of *De Trinitate*, book 8, he sets forth the famous notion that human love is a "trace" (*vestigium*) of the Trinity: "Love is of some one that loves, and with love something is loved. Behold, then, there are three things: he that loves, and that which is loved, and love."[124] He then carries this argument into book 9, expounding on the famous biblical predication, "God is love" (1 John 4:16).[125]

Augustine tells us that love consists of three dimensions: the lover, the beloved, and the act of love. Hegel's subject-object-act trinity reduces the divine to logical moments in historical process. The original subject-object-act triad in Augustine, by contrast, provides the ground for the aseity of the triune God: God does not need an other outside of himself in order to be love. Indeed, God does not need an other in order to be what he is. He is triune, and as such he can love, be loved, and be the very act of love in his simple, immutable, yet diverse and dynamic being.

The rest of book 9 of Augustine's *De Trinitate* applies the subject-object-act triad to the notion of knowledge, claiming that human self-knowledge, like self-love, is a vestige of the Trinity made in the image of God.[126] Augustine can therefore speak of the one divine substance in terms of *ad intra* relations such

---

123. Augustine, *On the Trinity*, ed. Philip Schaff, trans. Arthur West Haddan (Edinburgh: T. & T. Clark, 1887), 101.
124. Ibid., 124.
125. Ibid., 126.
126. Ibid., 126–33.

as love and knowledge. This enables him to make predications about God, and once God is a subject that can be predicated, he can break free from the Platonist tradition and speak of God as a being.

There is, of course, still a suspiciously Platonist element in Augustine's ontology. The *vestigium trinitatis* and the Platonist language of participatory "image" seem to suggest that there is some sort of a substantial continuity between the divine attributes and the natures with which God endowed the creatures. God created everything out of nothing, and surely Augustine would say that the "*ex nihilo*" refers to both forms and matter. However, the *vestigium trinitatis* seems to suggest that the forms did not come from nothing, but overflowed from the inward nature of God. This ontological continuity between God and creatures was strengthened when medieval scholastics like Thomas Aquinas incorporated Aristotelian metaphysics into Christian ontology and identified God as the first cause of the universe. As we have seen, this Aristotelian understanding of divine-human relations in terms of an analogy of being (*analogia entis*), when all its logical loose ends are tied, ultimately leads into a Hegelian type of monistic idealism.

In the history of Western theology, it was Calvin who severed this ontological connection between God and creatures to reiterate the Creator-creature distinction. Calvin makes an important distinction between primary and secondary causality. This is in fact a distinction that undergirds Calvin's understanding of God's activities in relation to the world. He writes in a 1558 treatise on providence: "I distinguish *everywhere* between primary and secondary causes and between mediate and proximate causes."[127] In his 1559 *Institutes*, Calvin explains that God's will is "the highest

---

127. John Calvin, *The Secret Providence of God*, trans. Paul Helm (Wheaton, IL: Crossway, 2010), 101. Emphasis added.

and first cause of all things because nothing happens except from his command."[128] He designates this "first/primary cause" variously as "remote," "mediate," and "hidden," and "secondary causes" as "proximate" and "intermediate." Under the rubric "No disregard of intermediate causes!" Calvin states that "a godly man will not overlook the secondary causes," which are causations within the natural order of God's creation.[129]

The all-important Calvinistic distinction between first and secondary causality has profound implications for ontological Creator-creature relations. Both Platonism and Aristotelianism, Augustine and Thomas, assert a kind of causal-ontological continuity between the Creator and the creature.[130] God and his work of creation are construed as merely the top of a chain of causes, and this construal is really a nascent form of Hegelian monism. In this analogical framework, God is seen as a cause in fundamentally the same metaphysical sense as causation in the natural order.

Calvin's distinction allows us to see God's work of creation as a cause that is fundamentally and ontologically different from natural causation. If we can attribute the word "cause" to both God's supernatural work *with* and *outside of time* and the operations of the natural world *in time*, it is because God's acts and works *ad extra* are free and perfect expressions of what he is *ad intra*. While Calvin still understands divine freedom in more voluntaristic terms, later mainstream Reformed orthodoxy would place greater emphasis on the perfect correspondence between God's inward being and his outward works. Bavinck and Van Til would then describe the correspondence between God's being and his handiwork in the framework of archetype-ectype relations that we explained earlier. This Reformed formulation

128. Calvin, *Institutes*, 1.16.8, 1:208.
129. Ibid., 1.17.9, 1:221.
130. See Spencer, *The Analogy of Faith*, 40.

reflects the most intimate relationship between God and his creation while safeguarding the strictest ontological distinction between the Creator and his creatures.

In Hegel's system, the universe *is* what God is. Reformed theology, however, consistently maintains that creation is God's own *expression* of what he is. The natural universe and its history as such are understood to be God's *self-revelation*, an *act ad extra* that is distinct from his being. Because the finite universe is an *ad extra* expression of what God is, what it reveals through its finitude cannot be exhaustively comprehended by the finite human mind: Reformed orthodoxy subscribes to the axiom that the finite is incapable of comprehending the infinite (*finitum non capax infiniti*).

Recall how the human incapacity to comprehend exhaustively its own nature and the universe implies that Hegel's philosophy is inevitably irrationalistic. In his monist system, there is no cognitive subject that knows reality exhaustively. There is thus no authoritative point of reference to which the human intellect can appeal for logical-systematic knowledge of the universe.

The Reformed doctrine of divine incomprehensibility, on the other hand, "presupposes that God is wholly known to himself and that he wholly knows his created world."[131] Sure enough, autonomous, unaided human reason is incapable of comprehending the mystery of God. "If man is to know about . . . [the] divine mind which stands above him as his Creator and therefore as his lawgiver, he will be dependent on this divine mind for a voluntary revelation of itself."[132] The universe is intelligible to the human mind if and only if it is a work of God's voluntary act of revelation. Thus Van Til: "The voluntary character of this revelation appears not only if and when this God speaks to man in a directly personal

---

131. Van Til, *Systematic Theology*, 294.
132. Ibid., 292.

way; it appears no less in every fact of the created universe. For the created universe itself owes its existence to a voluntary act of God. It is intelligible only if seen as such."[133]

The inherently revelatory character of all creaturely reality does not only mean that human beings are capable of knowing God and the universe truly and systematically, though not exhaustively. Because "every fact that confronts me is revelational," it is also true that no human being can escape the truth of God.[134] The Reformed formulation of the doctrine of divine incomprehensibility, then, "presupposes ... that man, as created by God in his image, does know and cannot help but know God."[135] Van Til aptly points out that this is precisely the *"alte Metaphysik"* (old metaphysics) to which Hegel, with his post-Kantian dichotomy between divine transcendence and knowability, is "averse."[136]

The gift of revelation, both in creation and in Scripture, means that human beings can "think God's thoughts after him."[137] With the "gift of logical manipulation that this Creator has given" to us, we can systematically perceive and understand the truth of the universe and its Creator.[138] But because of the abiding Creator-creature distinction, our systematic and true knowledge of God and his creation can be "at no point a direct replica" of the system in God's mind.[139] Our knowledge of God in relation to everything that is not God, however, "will at every point be analogical of the system of God."[140] This is not an analogy of *being*—it defies all ontological links between God's being and ours. It is rather an analogy that arises from the correspondence between

133. Ibid.
134. Ibid.
135. Ibid., 294.
136. Ibid.
137. Ibid., 292.
138. Ibid.
139. Ibid.
140. Ibid.

God's *opera ad intra* (inward and eternal acts of the triune God that contain all his attributes), which are necessary to his being, and his voluntary *opera ad extra*, which cause no alteration whatsoever to his inward being. We remain the creatures, and God the Creator; we the ectype, and God the archetype; our knowledge of God and of ourselves ectypal, and God's self-knowledge and knowledge of his creatures archetypal.

Furthermore, Reformed theology subscribes to the soteriological principle that fallen human beings cannot understand God's revelation (*homo peccator non capax verbi divini*). The apostle Paul makes it emphatically clear that although we knew God—we cannot escape this knowledge—we shun his manifested glory, which is made perspicuous everywhere in the universe, and our foolish hearts are darkened. This makes God's *verbal* and *propositional* revelation necessary for us to obtain true and salvific knowledge of him. With the inward illumination of the Holy Spirit, we recognize Scripture as God's Word, and we submit to its authority.

"Therefore when God tells me something that pertains directly to his own being apart from the world, I may repeat on the level of my experience the words that he has spoken."[141] Against the post-Kantian claim that our knowledge of God pertains exclusively to his works in history and that knowledge of his eternal being is impossible, the Reformed understanding of biblical revelation contends that we can actually know about God's transcendent being, because God has spoken to us verbally and propositionally. "When he, for instance, tells me that he has existed from all eternity before the foundation of the world, I may repeat his words and say 'God is eternal,'" even though "it is evident that God has, and I have not, grasped fully what God means."[142]

141. Ibid., 293.
142. Ibid.

Van Til thus states that the Reformed Christian is the true "rationalist" that Hegel sought, but failed, to be.[143] It is the Reformed understandings of the Creator-creature distinction, divine incomprehensibility, and revelation that enable true and systematic human knowledge of everything in relation to God, and God in relation to everything that is not God. Hegel does not have a concrete universal, in light of which to make sense of the universe, but the Christian does. The Christian can, on the basis of revelation, think God's thoughts after him. "God knows himself exhaustively, and I know him truly but not exhaustively. Moreover, what holds true of things that God tells me about himself holds true of everything God tells me about myself or the world."[144] Contrary to Hegel's false dichotomy between divine transcendence and knowability, then, the biblical doctrine of divine incomprehensibility does not destroy "the possibility of predication in any field whatsoever."[145] Rather, the doctrine of divine incomprehensibility, which presupposes both God's transcendence and his self-revelation, is there to safeguard the very rationality of the human mind and the possibility of human knowledge of God and the universe. God has spoken, and this means that what Hegel sought and failed to achieve can actually be accomplished, as long as we listen to God, repeat his words, and think his thoughts after him.

---

143. Ibid., 291. By "rationalism," Van Til does not mean the modern rationalist school, of course. He is referring to the philosophical position that human reason is capable of systematically logicizing reality and obtaining true knowledge of it.
144. Ibid., 293.
145. Ibid., 294.

GLOSSARY

Absolute, the. A term that Hegel assimilates to God, "the absolute" (*das Absolute*) is grammatically an adjectival noun (German) or a nominal adjective (English): it is an adjective used as a noun. In Hegel's usage, the nominal use of "absolute" indicates a subject-predicate reversal that subverts our customary way of thinking. For instance, we are accustomed to the predication "God is absolute." When the adjective here becomes the subject, and the subject the predicate, an interesting proposition arises: "The absolute is God." Because "absolute" is originally an adjective, it is devoid of meaning without corresponding subjects that it predicates. Indeed, Hegel frequently uses "absolute" as an adjective to describe subjects such as "spirit," which evolves into "absolute spirit" through the process of an objective-subjective-absolute triad. The absolute, in other words, is spirit fully actualized *qua* spirit. Furthermore, "the absolute" as an adjectival noun is meaningful only on the condition that it encompasses all possible subjects in the phenomenal world. In other words, it is not absolute *in itself* (*an sich*).

It *becomes* absolute only through the trinitarian process in which it first becomes *for itself* (*für sich*), and then becomes *in and for itself* (*an und für sich*). That is, the absolute, empty and void in itself, must become an adjectival subject that qualifies the whole of the phenomenal universe, and then, in the form of human consciousness, comes to know itself as the all-encompassing absolute. Hegel calls this knowledge "absolute knowledge."

Absolute Idealism. Hegel's use of the term "absolute" alludes to an ultimate, though not immediate, identity between God and the phenomenal universe. This form of idealism, devised by Hegel and Schelling, was a response to Kant's transcendental idealism, which posited an unbridgeable gap between the mind and the external world. What sets absolute idealism apart from transcendental idealism is that the former no longer posits a reality-in-itself (*an sich*) apart from the mind. For absolute idealism, the mind is everything, and everything is the mind. The thrust of this approach to metaphysics is an identification of the cognizant subject (human consciousness) with its object of cognition (absolute spirit, which encompasses the whole of reality). The whole of world history is a process in which spirit actualizes itself through the sum total of human consciousness in each stage of history. This philosophy of ultimate (and, in Schelling's case, a more direct and simpler) identity between spirit and human consciousness was intended to allow the absolute idealists to overcome the noumena-phenomena gulf in Kant's transcendental idealism, thus safeguarding the possibility of rational knowledge of the world and of God.

Abstract. An adjective describing empty and meaningless objects. See concrete universal.

Actuality/Actualization. Actuality (*Wirklichkeit*) is the fully developed form (*Gestalt*) of a subject, and actualization

(*Verwirklichung*) is the process of this development. Hegel equates the actual with the rational, and so the contingent and the irrational are merely appearances (*Erscheinungen*) that are in one sense without actuality. However, the contingencies in the appearance of a concept are also described as *immediate actualities*. Only through the stage of appearances can immediate actualities become *developed actualities*. Hegel equates the *truly actual*—the rational and the absolute in its fully developed moment, in which all contingencies have been expelled—with God.

Appearance. In most English translations of Hegel's works, "appearance" is a rendering of both *Schein* and *Erscheinung*. These are two distinct, though related, notions. (1) *Schein*. While the more colloquial usage of *Schein* carries the connotation of "illusion" (this is how Kant employs the term in the framework of his noumena-phenomena distinction), the corresponding verb *scheinen* means for Hegel the disclosure of an essence (*Wesen*) through hiddenness, akin to the Lutheran dialectic of the *Deus absconditus* (God hidden) and *Deus revelatus* (God revealed). *Schein*, then, is the existential veil through which an essence appears (*scheint*) phenomenally. Also see being and essence. (2) *Erscheinung*. Unlike *Schein*, *Erscheinung* does not involve hiddenness. In *Erscheinung*, concept or the rational discloses itself in its entirety, albeit in the representational form of phenomenal contingencies. In this sense, *Erscheinung* refers to the phenomenal world as a whole in different representational stages of history. *Erscheinung* is transient and must be sublated to give way to the next and higher stage of *Erscheinung*, before finally being sublated in the moment of the absolute.

Being. Hegel draws a distinction between *Wesen* (essence) and *Sein* (being). The German word *Wesen* is a direct rendering of the Latin philosophical term *essentia*, from *esse* (be), which has traditionally been used to denote the metaphysical concept of "being." In this more traditional usage, *Wesen* and *Sein* can be employed interchangeably to denote "being" in the sense of *essentia*. In Hegel's usage, however, an essence is the *conceptual* (see concept) underpinning of a thing: it is the determination of the thing as it really is in and for itself behind the veil of appearance (*Schein*). Being, by contrast, is the essence of a thing *as it appears* in its existential form, disclosed phenomenally through the veil of contingencies, transience, and irrationalities.

Concrete. The ultimate unity of particulars and universals, seen as an inseparable whole. See concrete universal.

Concrete Universal. In traditional metaphysics inherited from classical philosophy, abstract objects are usually associated with forms and universals. The *idea* of a mouse, for instance, is said to be abstract. Mickey, Jerry, Speedy, and Scratchy, on the other hand, are particulars within that universal species. Particulars are traditionally considered to be *concrete*. Hegel also contrasts the concrete to the abstract. He observes that universals, when abstracted from particulars, are nonexistent and devoid of content. The abstract as such denotes in Hegel's writings empty and meaningless objects. He applies the term "abstract" not only to universals detached from particulars, but also to particulars detached from universals. An *abstract particular* is a particular object severed from its defining idea. Without the species "mice" as its form, for instance, the name "Mickey" is but the empty name of an individual object that cannot be identified. The concrete, by contrast, means for Hegel the ultimate unity of particularity and universality, seen as an inseparable whole. He thus applies this term to particulars as well as universals. Universality develops into particularity, and then into individuality. In its fully actualized moment, the universal attains the form of concretion. The notion of a *concrete universal* is especially groundbreaking. It refers to the organic unity of every particular thing, and it makes every particular meaningfully related to all others. In other words, only in light of the concrete universal does this world of particular phenomena become meaningful to its cognizant observer. The term "concrete universal" has been critically adopted by Van Til to refer to the triune God and his will for the universe.

Concept. An important distinction in Hegel's speculative method is that between "concept" (*Begriff*) and "representation" (*Vorstellung*). Representational thinking is a form of understanding associated with sensibility, whereas conceptual thinking is to grasp the rational essence of something (the German word *Begriff* comes from the verb *greifen*, which literally means "to grasp" and figuratively refers to comprehensive knowledge). For Hegel, the rational is what is necessarily true and real; it is the "pure essentiality" of a thing. He does not deny the importance of *abstract* thinking and logic, but he insists that the whole truth of this pure essentiality is knowable to us only as it actualizes itself in historical reality. In actual history, however, a concept unavoidably takes on representational forms that carry contingent and accidental properties.

Consciousness. While the more colloquial usage of the word refers to a conscious state of mind, Hegel uses "consciousness" (*Bewußtsein*) to refer to the purposive intent of a subject towards an object. Furthermore, as an idealist, Hegel (as well as Kant) equates the consciousness of a subject to the conscious subject itself. In the *Science of Logic*, Hegel famously defines consciousness as "spirit as concrete, self-aware knowledge."

Cultivation. An overarching theme in Hegel's writings, *Bildung* (cultivation) comes from the noun *das Bild*, which means "picture" or "image." In its modern usage, this word usually refers to "education" in the broader sense of inculturation and social formation, and not just institutional schooling (*Erziehung*). The interesting association between "image" and "education" has its roots in medieval German mysticism, in which believers were taught to meditate on religious images for the purpose of spiritual formation. In the long nineteenth century, the notion of *Bildung* became a core value of German culture, and refers broadly to mental growth, personal formation, education, and inculturation. Hegel uses *Bildung* as an organic metaphor (see organicism) to refer to both personal cultivation and the developmental progress of spirit through the process of world history.

Determination/Determinacy. The German word for the Hegelian term "determination" (*Bestimmung*) is derived from "voice" (*Stimme*). For Fichte, the standard English translation of *Bestimmung* is "vocation." In a somewhat oversimplified way, we might understand Hegel's use of the noun as the *definition* of a substance understood in Hegelian terms as living subject. It is a dialectical notion with which Hegel replaces or fleshes out the more statically substantialist conception of nature or essence. The dialectical characteristic of *Bestimmung* means that a thing is *determinate* (*bestimmt*) only in relation to an other in the dialectical process of sublation. Hegel speaks of self-determination and means by it the autonomous disclosure of something's own essence by negating its present form and lifting itself up to a higher form of appearance.

Dialectic. (1) Dialectical Method. The word "dialectic" originated from a Greek verb that simply means "to converse with," which is also where the English word "dialogue" comes from. The Latin transliteration *dialectica* comes from a Greek term involving the word for "conversation" to refer to the philosophical art of debate. Dialectics, then, is simply a manner of philosophical investigation that seeks to uncover the truth through a process of debate between opposing voices. Hegel's dialectical method is characteristically modern in that his treatment of the science of logic challenges the law of non-contradiction. He does not simply dispense with the law of non-contradiction (or the laws of identity and of the excluded middle, for that matter). Yet he argues that truth is much more complex than can be accounted for by the traditional laws of logic. When we acknowledge the truth as the whole of a developmental process, says Hegel, we learn to come to terms with contradictions. One very helpful way to understand his dialectical method, then, is to see it as a presentation of the whole truth by the mediation of contradictions. (2) The Dialectical (moment of logic). In a narrower sense, the term "dialectical" refers specifically to the second moment of logic. Hegel describes it as "the negatively rational" (see negation/negativity). "Dialectical" in this sense connotes "self-contradictory." In the dialectical moment of logic, abstract understandings of universal forms, substances, etc., that are statically eternal are negated and thought to be nonexistent. The sublation of the dialectical leads to the third moment of logic, in which the truth as a whole is comprehended in terms of the process of its development as a subject.

Empiricism. The school of philosophy featuring the central epistemological tenet that sensory experience is the primary or even only source of human knowledge. Radical implementation of this tenet would theoretically amount to a denial of the possibility of metaphysics (at least that of a speculative sort), as is the case with David Hume (1771–76). Forerunners and earlier proponents of modern empiricism include British thinkers such as Francis Bacon (1561–1626), John Locke (1632–1704), and George Berkeley (1685–1753).

Essence. The determination of a thing by what it has in it to become ultimately; what a thing really is in and for itself behind the veil of appearance (*Schein*). See being.

Historicism. Originally a term coined by Hegel's contemporary, Friedrich Schlegel (1772–1829), "historicism" (*Historismus*) refers generally to philosophical views that describe history as purposive activity. The dialectical view of history developed by Hegel and espoused by various forms of Hegelianism is among the most influential—arguably *the* most influential—versions of historicism developed in the long nineteenth century. Hegel's historicism comprises a sociopolitical dimension and a metaphysical one. He envisions a future in which a perfect state emerges to serve as the bedrock of human freedom, and identifies the full actualization of this freedom as the final purpose of history. This is the stage of history in which spirit becomes the truly actual and enters into the moment of the absolute. Left-Hegelian and post-Kantian interpreters tend to downplay or even deny the metaphysical dimension, either by criticizing it as an inconsistency in Hegel's thought or by treating it as merely metaphoric. Traditionalist and revised-metaphysical interpreters, by contrast, identify the purposive activity of spirit as the driving force of social changes that take place in the phenomenal sphere.

Idea. While "idea" in the traditional Platonic sense is immutable and transcendent to the world, in Hegel's usage it refers to reality in the moment of the positively rational, in which its essence is fully manifested. This reality is spirit reconciled to itself and thus *in and for itself*. "Idea" is in this sense synonymous with "the absolute."

Immediacy. A term borrowed from German romanticism, "immediacy" means "without reflection." Hegel ascribes immediacy to the moment of abstraction prior to subject-object differentiation (see logic). Immediacy is opposed to mediation, which encompasses differentiation and reconciliation.

Individuality. The result of the reconciliation of particularity to universality. See concrete universal.

Infinite. Infinity refers to the unconditionedness in which a thing is no longer defined or confined by external, phenomenal, representational factors. Something is infinite if and only if it is positively rational (i.e., its concept is fully actualized); it is finite insofar as it is still representational. "Infinite" is thus a predicate of the absolute.

Mediation. According to Hegel, the truth is a process of mediation, which he opposes to immediacy. Immediacy is the stage in which the truth is expressed merely as abstract universals. It is the moment in which spirit is only *in itself* (*an sich*), but without itself as a differentiated object. The process of self-objectification, represented by the Trinitarian doctrine of the eternal generation of the Son, allows spirit to be *for itself* (*für sich*). In this second moment, spirit becomes an other (*Anderssein*) to itself, which gives rise to self-contradiction and conflict. A third moment is necessary to complete the process of the development of the whole truth—the process of mediation. This moment is represented by the Trinitarian doctrine of the procession of the Holy Spirit, which allows spirit to be both *in and for itself* (*an und für sich*), and thus to be what it is essentially, namely, the absolute.

Metaphysics. The study of the first principles underlying reality. The questions that metaphysics seeks to address include the existence and nature of God, the origin and nature of the universe and of humankind, and being and becoming. In a narrower sense, metaphysics is the philosophical enterprise that, on assumption of intrinsic connections or correspondences between the human mind and the supposedly intelligible realities above and behind the sensible world, seeks to speculatively uncover the ultimate truth(s) of the universe. Metaphysics has traditionally been considered the central discipline of philosophy, but the legitimacy of metaphysical inquiries has been placed under severe scrutiny after David Hume. Immanuel Kant declared the unviability of traditional metaphysics, which found its basis in the realm of pure reason, but he also attempted to provide a new approach to this branch of philosophy by resorting to the realm of practical morality. Traditional- and revised-metaphysical Hegel scholars interpret his works as a modern attempt to revive speculative metaphysics.

Logic. Hegel assigns to "logic" ("the logical", "the Logic") the basic delimitation of "everything logically real," that is, "every concept or ... everything true in general." According to Hegel's system, then, logic and reality are inseparable. This stands in sharp contrast to the Aristotelian view according to which logic pertains to the mind of the cognizant subject and not external reality. Whereas Aristotelianism sees logic as philosophical *method* rather than philosophy proper, Hegel thinks that the method and content of philosophy are an inseparable whole. For Hegel, the logical consists of three moments, namely, (1) "the side of abstraction or of the understanding," (2) "the dialectical or negatively rational side," and (3) "the speculative or positively rational one." This Hegelian view of logic does not dispense with the axiomatic laws of logic in the Aristotelian paradigm, namely, the laws of non-contradiction, identity, and the excluded middle. Yet Hegel argues that the concept of truth is much more complex than can be accounted for by the traditional laws of logic. When we acknowledge the truth as the whole of a developmental process, says Hegel, we learn to come to terms with contradictions that are to be sublated only in and by the third moment of logic.

Moment. The word "moment" here is a direct translation of the German word *Moment*, the denotations of which are broader than its English equivalent. *Moment* can refer to a moment in time, but it can also designate "element" or "factor." Hegel's usage carries all these significations. The three moments of logic are *elements* of the same reality, though not as parts of the whole; rather, each moment *is* the whole of the same reality in different dimensions. Here Hegel is applying Trinitarian patterns of thinking to his understanding of logic. Unlike the coeternity of the three persons of the Godhead, as stated in traditional Christian doctrine, however, Hegel's logical trinity consists of the temporal process of successive moments developed through the course of history. See logic.

Monism. The philosophy or worldview which holds that the whole of reality ultimately consists of one and the same substance. Hegel's philosophy is often described as monistic, especially on traditional metaphysical interpretations, according to which the German philosopher sees the whole of the universe as one substantially divine subject.

Negation/Negativity. Hegel sometimes uses "negative" as a synonym of "dialectical." Negativity entails an object of negation. The negation of objectivity or objective truths is only a penultimate stage or moment in the dialectical process of mediation. The sublation, sometimes understood as "the negation of negation," of the negatively rational leads to the positively (existentially) rational, in which the whole of the truth is comprehended as one living subject reconciled to itself. In this dialectical scheme, negativity can be thought of as unactualized potentiality.

Object. In Hegel's writings, there are two words of which the standard English translation is "object." (1) *Objekt* refers generally to what the English word "object" designates. As such, an *Objekt* can be either actual or nonactual (see actuality). (2) *Gegenstand*, composed of *gegen* (against) and *Stand* (stand), denotes an object that, figuratively speaking, stands over against a subject. As such, *Gegenstand* refers to an object that is actual. Hegel often uses *Gegestand* to refer to the object of negation.

Organicism. Organicism refers generally to the kind of philosophy that treats reality and the truths concerning reality as an organic whole, akin to a living organism, the constituent parts of which are biologically interrelated in such a way that together they sustain the life of the organism and contribute to its growth. Understood organically, propositional truths are valid, not as abstract propositions that are true in themselves, but as truthful predications about reality likened in one way or another to a living subject. Organicism is thus characterized by the use of *organic metaphors* as a key to interpreting reality and the truths concerning it. Hegel sees the whole of the universe as one living substance or subject undergoing organic development through time in a dialectical manner.

Panentheism. The German philosopher Karl Krause (1781–1832) coined the term "panentheism" specifically to distinguish Hegel's (and Schelling's) supposedly metaphysical system from pantheism. Whereas pantheism asserts that God and the universe are *simpliciter* identical, panentheism contends that the two are *ultimately*, but not *immediately*, one. For Hegel (as understood by traditional and revised metaphysical interpreters), the phenomenal world is *essentially* divine, but its historical appearance also exhibits irrationalities and contingencies that contradict its divine essence. Accordingly, God and the universe are not immediately identical, but they become and are identical through the process of mediation.

Pantheism. Pantheism refers generally to the view that all reality is inherently divine, or that divinity pervades everything in the universe. Accordingly, there is no God transcendent to, or deity distinct from, the world. Bavinck and Van Til describe Hegel as a pantheist, though panentheism may be a more accurate description of his philosophical system.

Particularity. See concept and concrete universal.

Positivity. In simple terms, by "positive" Hegel means "existent" or "existential." On its own, "positivity" can refer to sheer existence as opposed to rationality. Something can also be "positively rational" (see logic), which is to say that its positivity and rationality are reconciled (i.e., its rationality is existentially or positively actualized).

Post-Kantian/Nonmetaphysical Interpretation of Hegel. One influential view of Hegel has held that at the heart of his highly metaphysical philosophy is Kant's antimetaphysical critique of reason. In more recent English-language scholarship, some have carried the theme of the continuity between Hegel and Kant even further. The so-called post-Kantian interpreters have made the controversial claim that Hegel never taught the kind of traditionalistic metaphysics described by the traditionalist interpreters, and that he consistently subscribed to Kant's antimetaphysical critique of reason throughout his career. On this view, Hegel's idealism is understood as an advancement of Kant's critical philosophy, registering critical corrections of Kant on the basis of his own critique, thus completing Kant's intellectual revolution by purifying it of the remaining vestiges of traditional metaphysics. Also see traditionalist/traditional metaphysical and revised/critical metaphysical interpretations of Hegel.

Process Philosophy. The philosophical view that *becoming* takes ontological priority over *being*. Opposed to substance metaphysics. Hegel's absolute idealism is often understood to be the fountainhead of modern process philosophy. According to Hegel, the essence of a thing is not determined by what that thing *is* now, that is, the way the thing appears in its current form. Rather, the essence of a thing is what determines how the thing has *become* what it is at present, which is the same as what it has in it to *become* ultimately.

Rationalism. The school of philosophy characterized by its central epistemological tenet that reason, rather than experience, is the foundation of knowledge. Rationalism holds that rational certainty about our thought processes (such as innate concepts, innate knowledge, and intuition-deduction processes) provides the ground whereupon we can make sense of the external world. Rationalist metaphysics presupposes certain correspondences between the metaphysical order of the external world and the analytical order of our mental processes. Representatives of modern rationalism include Continental philosophers such as René Descartes (1596–1650), Baruch Spinoza (1632–77), G. W. Leibniz (1646–1716), and Christian Wolf (1679–1754).

Rationality/Reason. For Hegel, rationality entails not only order, but also purposive activity. Reality is rational, but not just because it is naturally embedded with rational order. Reality has a mind of its own that is purposive in its developmental process. The purpose of reason, be it that of spirit or of human consciousness, is to comprehend the rationality of reality speculatively.

Reconciliation. A term borrowed from Christian theology, "reconciliation" (*Versöhnung*) in Hegel's usage describes the union between human consciousness and spirit. He does not think of humankind's alienation from God as a result of some offence against him. Rather, God and humankind are ultimately identical as one spirit, and so this alienation is spirit's self-alienation. Spirit alienates itself from itself, in order to reconcile itself to itself. Hegel's notion of reconciliation is primarily *ontological* and derivatively *ethical* in a sociopolitical sense. Ontological alienation manifests itself existentially in the problematic features of social reality, and the speculative philosopher must recognize that the human plight at present will eventually be sublated by the process of reconciliation. Hegel himself puts it rather poetically in a famous line from his preface to the *Philosophy of Right*: "To recognize reason as the rose in the cross of the present and thereby to delight in the present—this rational insight is the *reconciliation* with actuality."

Religion. Hegel thinks of religion as a representation of the philosophical concept of God, which he identifies as the truly actual and rational, the absolute, the absolute spirit that comprehends its essence. Scholars who tend to steer away from theological interpretations of Hegel usually understand his "God" as some kind of cosmic logic that underpins the evolutionary process of the universe. In any case, Hegel calls Christianity the "consummate religion" because its theological representations, especially the doctrines of the Trinity, the incarnation, and reconciliation, closely manifest the conceptual content of his philosophical system. In his earlier writings, Hegel envisions a future stage of history in which religion, including Christianity, is sublated to give way to philosophy. In his 1827 *Lectures on the Philosophy of Religion*, however, Hegel observes that philosophers will always be among the minority, and contends that Christianity in its consummate form as a *"people's religion"* (*Volksreligion*) will always continue to be necessary in this world to teach the truth of reconciliation in representational form accessible to the common folk. Some scholars (e.g., Thomas Lewis) have even argued that for Hegel, Christianity as a *Volksreligion* has a kind of cohesive function in modern society that undergirds the values of right (*Recht*: this word refers broadly to "right," as in "human rights" and what is morally "right," as well as "law"), freedom, and peace.

Representation. Representational thinking is a form of understanding associated with sensibility. Representation (*Vorstellung*) is contrasted to and used in conjunction with concept; it is phenomenal and carries accidental qualities.

Revised/Critical Metaphysical Interpretation of Hegel. The highly controverted assertions made by the post-Kantian interpreters, though difficult to accept for those who take Hegel's texts at face value, have at least successfully called attention to the strong Kantian influences that can be discerned in his writings. This has forced the traditionalist interpreters of Hegel to revise their own views accordingly. The "revised metaphysical" or "critical metaphysical" interpreters believe that it is most reasonable to acknowledge both the Kantian-critical aspect of Hegel's philosophical method and his textually evident attempts to rescue religion and traditional metaphysics. See also post-Kantian/nonmetaphysical and traditionalist/traditional metaphysical interpretations of Hegel.

Speculation. Hegel describes his own philosophy and philosophical method as "speculative," a term that has a number of connotations on top of its denotation. In a more general sense, the term refers to the speculative approach to metaphysics handed down from Plato and Aristotle to Descartes, Spinoza, and Leibniz. This tradition, which Hegel describes as having been renounced and extirpated by Kantian philosophy, assumes that there is an intrinsic connection or correspondence between the human mind and external reality in such a way that we can make sense of the world on the basis of rational speculation. Hegel's own speculative philosophy or method of speculation presupposes that the whole of reality is a living subject going through the purposive process of mediation, and that human consciousness is ultimately identical to spirit.

Spirit. Spirit (*Geist*, rendered as "mind" in older English translations) is what the truth of the universe is as a living subject. As such, it undergoes different moments and takes on different forms. *Subjective spirit* is spirit in the form of individual consciousness. *Objective spirit* is the collective consciousness of society manifested in the form of culture and customs. Consciousness is spirit that thinks its essence, and in the ultimate moment of this speculative process, spirit comes to comprehend itself as what it truly is in essence, namely, absolute spirit or spirit as the absolute.

Sublation. The idiosyncrasy of this term in English reflects Hegel's unique use of the German word *Aufhebung*, which some English-speaking scholars prefer to render as "supersession." The German verb *heben* means "to lift," and *aufheben* in its ordinary usage can mean either "to cancel/abrogate" or "to lift up/elevate." Hegel combines both denotations of *aufheben* to refer to the abrogation or negation of a previous moment of logic—not for the purpose of annihilating it, but rather to elevate it to the next, positive moment. On this view, in its narrower sense "sublation" refers to the second, negative moment of logic, namely, the negation of the first moment. In its broader sense, however, the three-moment dialectic as a whole can be described as a process of sublation. In this sense, "sublation" can be understood as the negation of negation for the purpose of elevation towards the positive.

Substance Metaphysics/Substantialism. A term used by proponents of process philosophy and twentieth-century phenomenological philosophy, substance metaphysics or substantialism refers to the view that the substance (or substances) constituting the whole of reality is, in Hegelian terms, a statically "abstract universality" characterized by "bare uniformity"—i.e., "undifferentiated, unmoved substantiality." Hegel does not deny that the truth has such a substantial dimension, but this alone is not the whole truth. He proposes to understand reality as a historical *process* unfolding itself through dialectical stages; hence, the term "process philosophy" is frequently applied to his system. Soviet philosophers, whose dialectical materialist view of history can be traced back to the Left Hegelians and even to Hegel himself, use "substance metaphysics" or "substantialism" in a different way to designate all philosophical views asserting that substantial realities underlie phenomena. In this tradition, "substantialism" and "idealism" are often used synonymously. On the dialectical materialist view, then, Fichte's "ego," Hegel's "absolute spirit," Locke's "substratum," and even Democritus's "atom" are all derogatively labelled "substantialist" and thus "idealist."

Truth as Subject. According to Hegel, the truth of the universe is not merely an unchanging set of abstract forms; it is a living subject as well. Life is a process, and to say that the ultimate truth is a living subject is to say that it manifests itself through the process of its life. This means that even in its substantial moment, the subject is not a dead, static, abstract substance, but "living substance."

Traditionalist/Traditional Metaphysical Interpretation of Hegel. The older, mainstream interpretation of Hegel, which sees him as reacting against Kant to recover the science of metaphysics as traditionally understood. On this view, the identification of God as absolute spirit lies at the very heart of Hegel's metaphysics. The mind of God expresses and actualizes itself through the historical process of the development of the collective consciousness of his creatures. This means that we can come to know the ultimate reality of the mind of God through the philosophical study of the history of human consciousness. Also see post-Kantian/nonmetaphysical and revised/critical metaphysical interpretations of Hegel.

Transcendental Idealism. The form of idealism espoused by Immanuel Kant (1724–1804), the difficulties of which Hegel's *absolute idealism* seeks to overcome. Kant's definition of *idealism* is largely negative: an idealist is one who *denies* that the reality of sensible objects can be ascertained by immediate perception or experience, and thus posits that reality is intelligible only by other means. There are several schools of idealism offering different accounts of how the cognizant self can cognize the world, and the term *transcendental*, in Kant's own words, refers to the way in which "we cognize that and how certain representations . . . are applied entirely *a priori*, or are possible." His transcendental method as such posits that the possibility of sensory experience rests on certain active categories of the mind. In particular, space and time are not real things in themselves, nor are they appearances of things that we intuit. Rather, they are the very form of our intuition: they are part and parcel of the mental process by which we cognize external objects as they appear to us (phenomena)—not as they are in themselves (noumena). Because our sensory perception can cognize objects only in space and time, this form of intuition—an active process on the part of the cognizant subject—is a necessary precondition for external things to appear to us. This means that as subjects of cognition, we are not merely passive receivers of sensory data external to us. Our minds play an active organizing role in perceiving and understanding the appearances of objects external to us. Transcendental idealism, then, presupposes an unbridgeable gap between noumena and phenomena as a result of the separation between the human mind and external things, which renders what Hegel calls "speculative" metaphysics impossible.

Worldview. The use of the term "worldview" (*Weltanschauung*) in German idealism is rooted in the Kantian notion of "intuition" (*Anschauung*), which, in simple terms, refers to the immediate cognitive perception of a phenomenon. Hegel uses "worldview" to refer generally to intuitive ways in which people interpret the phenomenal world with preconceived presuppositions of which they are often unaware. He thinks that an important task of philosophy is to analyze the structures of various worldviews, especially as they relate to religious convictions, in order to resolve the theoretical contradictions in these structures that often manifest themselves in sufferings and social conflicts.

RECOMMENDED READING

As we have seen through the course of this book, Hegel's works are not at all easy to comprehend, and they have been subjected to many different interpretations. The implications of his philosophy have been carried to the left and to the right, politically. Liberal and conservative theologians have found different aspects of his thought appealing. Even twentieth-century New Confucianism found support in Hegel for its purpose of modernizing ancient Chinese philosophy. More recent scholars who try to take Hegel's words at face value without preconceived agendas have also found themselves in endless debates that do not seem resolvable in the near future. For this reason, it is almost impossible to offer an interpretation of Hegel that is entirely objective.

In this book, I have tried to offer a construal of Hegel's philosophical method by drawing on the least controverted aspects of his thought. Still, inevitably, I have had to rely on one interpretational model that I deem most balanced and objective, and arguably least controversial in the field of Hegel studies. When it comes to philosophical content, it becomes even harder to maintain this relative objectivity—and this has been the case with the section on Hegel's philosophy of religion.

It is therefore essential that readers who wish to go further in studying Hegel read for themselves the philosopher's primary texts, with the aid of other reliable introductory as well as secondary sources. I will not provide an exhaustive list of Hegel's works here (there are relatively few in fact), as such information can be easily accessed online. Rather, I shall suggest a plan for reading Hegel.

Primary Literature

I recommend that the reader begin with the preface and introduction to the *Phenomenology of Spirit*. This part is relatively easier to read (though some passages can still be quite challenging), and gives the reader a sense of the whole agenda of Hegel's subsequent writings. *Do not* read further in the *Phenomenology*, however. The reason is that Hegel would revise his views in his later works, and it would be undesirable for the reader to gain a preconceived framework from this earlier opus and impose it on Hegel's other writings. In fact, reading Hegel's other works in light of the *Phenomenology* has been a major source of interpretational mistakes in English-language Hegel studies, even at the scholarly level.

Skip instead to the first volume of the *Encyclopedia of the Philosophical Sciences*, often referred to as the *Encyclopedia of Logic* (not to be confused with his other work, *The Science of Logic*, of which the first volume of the *Encyclopedia* is an abridged version). This is a must-read before proceeding to Hegel's other works, for it spells out the basic method described in the preface to the *Phenomenology* in clear and systematic details.

Do not finish reading the whole *Encyclopedia* at this step, either. Turn to the posthumously published lectures that Hegel delivered during the final stage of his career in Berlin. Start with the *History of Philosophy*, followed by the *Philosophy of Religion*, *Philosophy of History*, and then *Aesthetics*. Instead of reading through all the materials, however, just read the introductions. After this, the big picture is basically complete. *Do not* attempt to read through the entire volumes upon first reading: you need the big picture first.

As a last step, return to the *Encyclopedia* and read the second and third volumes on the philosophy of nature and the philosophy of mind/spirit, respectively (the three volumes are published under separate titles by Oxford University Press). After that, you should be able to read with a firm foundation any other work by Hegel that interests you.

Introductory and Secondary Literature

There is a wealth of introductory and secondary literature on Hegel out there. If the reader starts reading them randomly, confusion will most likely follow, instead of clarification, even if they are good books. Again, the reader needs a map to steer through the literature on Hegel. There are just too many good books out there, so for each genre I will pick only one that I have personally found helpful.

1. Craig Matarrese, *Starting with Hegel* (Continuum, 2010). As an initial step, I suggest that the reader begin with an introduction that traces the development of Hegel's thought, instead of one that focuses on one of his major works or on the overarching themes of his system. I wish I could have done that in this book, but given its prescribed length, that would have been an unrealistic goal. Thankfully, Craig Matarrese has written a highly accessible book of this sort—only 170 pages in length. Again, even with books like this, it is inevitable that some of the

things the author says will turn out to be controversial among Hegel scholars, so it is crucial that the reader always keep an open and critical mind when reading these materials.

2. Jon Stewart, ed., *The Hegel Myths and Legends* (Northwestern University Press, 1996). One of the household names in the study of modern philosophy in America (best known for his works on Søren Kierkegaard), Jon Stewart is the editor of this classic for beginners in Hegel studies. The book addresses virtually all of the most important themes in Hegel's writings that have often been misinterpreted. The contributors make up an all-star team, consisting of some of the most venerated names in the field (although many have been left out). The multiple scholarly voices that this book includes give to it a richness and diversity of views that single-author books cannot achieve. Together, these contributors debunk such myths as the "thesis-antithesis-synthesis" triad commonly, but falsely, attributed to Hegel. This book is written at the level of an undergraduate textbook, so it is slightly more difficult than the previous recommendation, but it should still be manageable.

3. Terry Pinkard, *Hegel: A Biography* (Cambridge University Press, 2001). While biographies generally tend to be a more objective genre than interpretations of a thinker's thought, this is curiously not the case with Hegel. There has yet to be a biography of Hegel that satisfies every scholar. Pinkard's view of Hegel is representative of the controversial "post-Kantian" school of interpretation, and this inevitably affects his decisions on which materials to use and which to neglect. Even so, I have found that Pinkard's portrait of Hegel is more complete than other biographies. This book is especially helpful in situating Hegel within the spirit of his age.

4. Dean Moyar and Michael Quante, eds., *Hegel's Phenomenology of Spirit: A Critical Guide* (Cambridge University Press, 2008). With the previous warning not to interpret Hegel's system through the lens of the *Phenomenology*, we also need to bear in mind that as far as influence is concerned, this monumental work eclipses all his other works, including the *Encyclopedia*. The book edited by Moyar and Quante gives us a critical understanding of the significance of the *Phenomenology* beyond Hegel studies. This is another all-star performance, in which leading Hegel scholars come at the subject from multiple angles, giving the reader a bird's-eye view of the place of Hegel's early *magnum opus* in the broad history of thought and culture.

5. Stephen Houlgate, *The Opening of Hegel's Logic: From Being to Infinity* (Purdue University Press, 2005). This book is for more advanced readers at the graduate school level (e.g., graduate school students in philosophy or seminary students writing Master of Theology theses in the field of modern theology). In English-language Hegel studies, one major ongoing controversy has focused on the role of Kant's influence on Hegel. Houlgate takes a middle position, drawing insights from both the "traditional metaphysical" and the "post-Kantian" sides, while remaining critical of both. Although I am in no position to say which of these interpretations is the right one, the relatively more balanced reading that Houlgate represents gives us a helpful way into the controversy by evaluating the strengths and weaknesses of both sides.

6. Michael Inwood, *A Hegel Dictionary* (Wiley-Blackwell, 1992). Hegel is notorious for his idiosyncratic use of German words, and English translations of his technical terms often tend to bewilder the reader even more than the original language. For

readers beginning with Hegel's primary texts, this dictionary would certainly be immensely helpful.

7. Dean Moyar, ed., *The Oxford Handbook of Hegel* (Oxford University Press, 2017). As with any other volume in the *Oxford Handbooks* series, this is the most comprehensive and authoritative guide to the subject. This volume covers major topics in Hegel studies by dividing them according to his major works in chronological order. The authors of the thirty-four chapters include established scholars and rising stars in Hegel studies. As a reference work accessible to average undergraduate students, this collection of essays is, in my view, the best way to gain a sense of what Hegel studies is all about in our day and age. (I also recommend the 2006 *Cambridge Companion to Hegel* and the 2008 *Cambridge Companion to Hegel and Nineteenth-Century Philosophy*, both edited by Frederick Beiser, although these are much more technical and less up-to-date than the *Oxford Handbook*.)

INDEX OF SCRIPTURE

Genesis
1:1—78
1:20–24—57

Exodus
3:14—78, 121

Deuteronomy
29:29—123–24

John
4:24—78

Acts
17:23—71
17:28—71

Romans
1:18–32—69–70
1:18–21—71

1 Corinthians
13:1—117

Ephesians
1:23—50
4:4–6—50
4:11–13—50
4:15–16—50
5:21–23—51

Philippians
2:7—103

1 Peter
3:15—4

1 John
1:5—78
4:8—78
4:16—78, 122

INDEX OF SUBJECTS AND NAMES

apologetics
  cultural, 94–95
  presuppositional, 87, 97
Aristotelianism, 15, 33, 45, 47, 52, 87, 98–102, 110, 121, 123
Aristotle, 10, 14–15, 28, 32–33, 45, 47–48, 51–52, 57, 87–88, 98–99, 101, 110, 121
atheism, 6, 68, 73, 75
Augustine, 15, 64, 98, 117–24

Bacon, Francis, 16
Barth, Karl, 8–9, 23, 98, 102–3, 112
Bauer, Bruno, 30, 113
Bavinck, Herman, 9, 51, 68–70, 72–76, 78, 81, 83–84, 87–88, 90, 92, 94, 96, 106, 109–12, 114–17, 124
Berkeley, George, 16
Bloch, Ernst, 6
Bultmann, Rudolf, 8

Calvin, John, 3, 10, 69–70, 101, 119, 123–24
Christology, 81–82, 106, 115
  Chalcedonian, 77, 81
  communication of attributes, 82
concrete universal, 86, 88–90, 92–94, 107, 116, 128, 130, 132–33
consciousness, 22, 34–35, 37, 40, 54–55, 58, 60–65, 80, 89, 95–96, 107–8, 110–16
creatio ex nihilo, 117–20, 123

Creator-creature distinction, 73, 79, 81, 84, 101, 104, 106, 117, 119, 122–23, 126, 128
cultivation (*Bildung*), 50, 53–56, 63, 66

deism, 85, 114
Derrida, Jacques, 6
Descartes, René, 10, 15, 17, 32, 98, 118, 121
dialectical method, 6, 23, 43–45, 50
Dilthey, Wilhelm, 31

Edwards, Jonathan, 10
empiricism, 10–11, 16–18
Engels, Friedrich, 31
Enlightenment, 17, 25–26
epistemology, 16, 87

Feuerbach, Ludwig, 30, 67, 111–13, 115–16
Fichte, Johann Gottlieb, 17, 21, 30, 43, 110

God
    aseity of, 76, 91, 93, 117, 119–20, 122
    classical theism, 24, 99, 102–3
    eternality of, 49, 64, 67, 83–84, 104, 109, 114, 117, 119–20, 127
    immutability of, 83–84, 92, 99, 103, 105, 109, 117, 120–22
    impassibility of, 99, 103, 117

    simplicity of, 49, 64, 85, 92, 99, 109, 117, 120–22
    transcendence of, 24, 26, 81, 91, 104–5, 109–10, 114, 117, 120–21, 126–28

Harnack, Adolf von, 8
Hegel, Georg Wilhelm Friedrich, 1–12, 14, 17, 21–81, 83–91, 94–97, 99, 102, 104–8, 110–13, 115–17, 121–22, 125–26, 128
    interpretation of, 23–24, 28, 33, 47, 80–81, 85, 105, 110, 126–27
Hegelianism
    Left/Young, 6, 8, 62, 67, 113
    Right/Old, 111
Heidegger, Martin, 6
Herrmann, Wilhelm, 8
historicism, 39, 58, 94, 96
history, philosophy of, 30
Hodge, Charles, 9, 70
Hölderlin, Johann Christian Friedrich, 21, 25, 27–29
Hume, David, 10, 16–18

idealism
    British, 4–5
    German, 26, 77, 79
    transcendental, 11, 19–22, 25, 33, 35, 37
image of God, 50, 53, 113, 118, 122–23, 126
irrationalism, 106, 108, 116, 125

Kant, Immanuel, 1–3, 7–8, 17–23, 25, 28, 32–33, 35, 37, 45, 47, 67, 72, 81, 107, 110
Kierkegaard, Søren, 68, 107
Kuyper, Abraham, 9, 72, 97

Leibniz, Gottfried Wilhelm, 15, 17, 32
Locke, John, 10, 16
logic, 24, 31–36, 43–47, 50, 52, 56–60, 85, 88, 91, 96, 98–101, 108, 122
    of mediation, 43, 46, 49, 60, 83, 89

Martensen, Hans Lassen, 68
Marxism, 1, 6
Marx, Karl, 6–7, 25, 31
materialism, 6, 68, 73–76, 112, 115–16
metaphysics, 2, 8, 14–18, 20–25, 28, 32–34, 44–45, 47, 52, 73–74, 85, 87, 95, 98–102, 118, 123–24, 126
    classical, 28
Moltmann, Jürgen, 8, 102

neo-Calvinism, 3

Old Princeton, 3, 9
organicism, 50–52, 55, 59, 72–80, 82–87, 90, 108

pantheism, 74–75
phenomenology, 2, 12, 29–31, 46, 48, 50–52, 56, 61–63, 95, 107, 110
philosophy
    British, 4–5
    continental, 6, 16
    history of, 11, 24, 30, 37, 41, 98
    modern, 11, 15, 17–18, 24, 34, 37
Plato, 14, 28, 32, 41, 45, 52, 55, 87, 98–99, 108–10, 117–18, 120–21, 123
process metaphysics, 28, 40, 47, 51–52

rationalism, 11, 15–18, 21, 33, 51, 106, 108, 128
reconciliation, 41–43, 60, 63, 65–67, 111–12
Reformed orthodoxy, 10, 87, 97–100, 101, 124–25
religion
    consummate, Christianity as, 61–65, 112
    people's, 27, 67
    philosophy of, 30–31, 44, 61–62, 64, 67
revelation
    general, 69, 71
    perspicuity of, 127
    progressive, 82
    propositional, 78, 127
    special, 26, 82–84
Ritschl, Albrecht, 8
romanticism, 25, 27, 54

Sartre, Jean-Paul, 6
Schaeffer, Francis, 94–96
Schelling, Friedrich Wilhelm
   Joseph von, 17, 21–22, 24,
   26–29
Schleiermacher, Friedrich, 8, 21,
   26, 30, 32, 54, 111, 113
scholasticism, 15, 34, 87,
   98–102, 104
Scholten, Johannes, 9, 68
speculative method, 8, 11, 25,
   28, 31–37, 39–44, 46, 56,
   60, 91
Spinoza, Baruch, 15, 26, 32, 52
spirit
   absolute, 2, 22, 55, 60, 89
   for itself, 49, 53
   in and for itself, 49
   in itself, 19, 22, 49, 53, 85
   of the age, 27, 39, 95, 96
   self-alienation of, 42, 45, 49, 55
   self-differentiation of, 49, 64,
      121
   self-reconciliation of, 45, 55
Strauss, David Friedrich, 8, 30,
   111–17
sublation (*Aufhebung*), 44, 59,
   64–65
substance metaphysics, 28,
   47–48, 51–53, 58, 73, 83,
   87, 91, 94, 102

theology
   biblical, 77, 79, 81, 86
   modern, 7, 9–10
   natural, 98–99, 101
   Reformed, 3, 5, 9–10, 12, 14,
      72, 78, 80, 94, 104, 117,
      119, 125, 127
Thomism, 10, 101, 121, 123–24
Trinity, 64, 68, 73, 76, 90,
   92–94, 102–3, 105, 119,
   122, 127
   economic, 104
   logical, 57, 68, 76, 121

University of Berlin, 8, 30, 111

Van Til, Cornelius, 1, 3–5,
   69–70, 72, 77, 86, 88–94,
   96–97, 99–100, 102, 105–
   9, 116–17, 124–26, 128
Voetius, Gisbertus, 10
Vos, Geerhardus, 72, 77–86, 94,
   96

Weber, Max, 7, 31
Witsius, Herman, 10

Shao Kai ("Alex") Tseng (DPhil, Oxford) is research professor in the Department of Philosophy at Zhejiang University, China. His research publications have covered areas including modern theology, Continental philosophy, Reformed orthodoxy, Song-Ming Confucianism, and philosophy of music. He is the author of *G. W. F. Hegel* (2018) in the P&R Great Thinkers series, *Barth's Ontology of Sin and Grace: Variations on a Theme of Augustine* (2019), and *Karl Barth's Infralapsarian Theology: Origins and Development 1920–1953* (2016), and a contributor to the *Oxford Handbook of Nineteenth-Century Christian Thought* (2017) and *Blackwell Companion to Karl Barth* (forthcoming).

JOHN M. FRAME

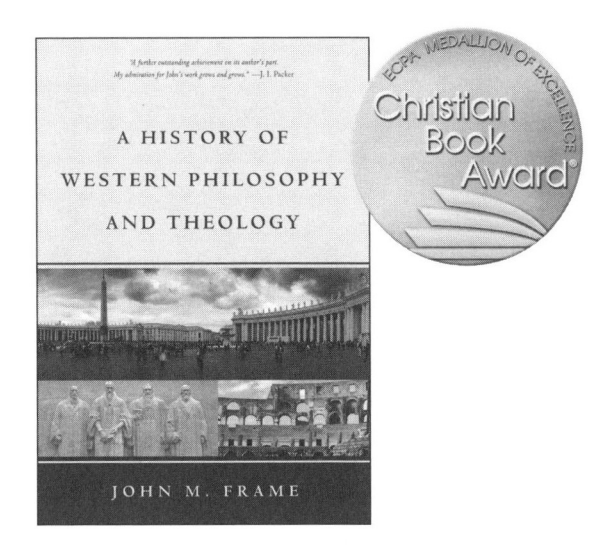

**Winner of the 2017 ECPA Gold Medallion Award
in the Bible Reference Works Category**

A History of Western Philosophy and Theology is the fruit of John Frame's forty-five years of teaching philosophical subjects. No other survey of the history of Western thought offers the same invigorating blend of expositional clarity, critical insight, and biblical wisdom. The supplemental study questions, bibliographies, links to audio lectures, quotes from influential thinkers, twenty appendices, and indexed glossary make this an excellent main textbook choice for seminary- and college-level courses and for personal study.

"This is the most important book ever written on the major figures and movements in philosophy. We have needed a sound guide, and this is it."
—**Vern S. Poythress,** Professor of New Testament, Westminster Theological Seminary